What to Say or Do...
From Diapers to Diploma

SECOND EDITION

What to Say or Do...

From Diapers to Diploma

A Parents' Quick Reference Guide

with an introduction by Kay Provine,
codeveloper of *Roots & Wings* parenting program

Illustrations by Patrice Barton

JOHNSON  INSTITUTE

HAZELDEN®

Hazelden
Center City, Minnesota 55012-0176

1-800-328-0094
1-651-213-4590 (Fax)
www.hazelden.org

Library of Congress Cataloging-in-Publication Data

What to say or do—from diapers to diploma : a parents quick
reference guide.
    p. cm.
  ISBN 1-56838-358-4 (pbk.)
  1. Child rearing—Handbooks, manuals, etc. 2. Parenting—
Handbooks, manuals, etc. I. Title: From diapers to diploma.
II. Johnson Institute (Minneapolis, Minn.)

HQ769 .W47 2000
649'.l—dc21   99-088165

04 03 02 01 00   6 5 4 3 2 1

Cover design by David Spohn
Illustrations by Patrice Barton
Interior design and typesetting by Spaulding & Kinne

Contents

SECTION 4: Ages 11–14

SECTION 5: Ages 15–18

Introduction

If you are raising a child (from toddler to teen) in the twenty-first century, *What to Say or Do* is here to help you. *What to Say or Do* offers support and field-tested ideas for responding effectively when your child's behavior concerns you.

We at Hazelden have been working with parents for years. I hope we have given new and useful information and strategies in our outreach and contact with parents, especially with the participants in *Roots & Wings: Raising Resilient Children,* one of our parenting programs. Delightfully, this program has been a two-way street. I have learned much from thousands of parents nationwide, in countless types of situations. Now, for the first time, the best of this exchange of information and ideas has been combined and organized for you in this handy book, *What to Say or Do.*

Many behaviors that concern us as parents can occur at more than one stage of a child's life. For simplicity, *What to Say or Do* covers each behavior at the age when parents most likely will encounter it in their child. We have grouped situations in the following age ranges: 2 to 4, 5 to 7, 8 to 10, 11 to 14, and 15 to 18. If the situation you need help with is not in the age group you expect, check one of the others. Something similar may be located in another age group.

For each behavior presented, you will find typical examples, to-the-point background information, and ideas about what to say or do to turn the problem behavior into a more desirable one. A Resolve and a Smart Tip are included to provide you with support as you tackle these difficult situations. We didn't want to overlook your stresses as a parent.

What to Say or Do contains the knowledge of parenting experts and the latest research on parenting. More important, it presents the experience of parents who have been in the trenches and raised children successfully, using good sense, practical approaches, loving firmness, and a big dose of humor. It is my hope that this book accurately reflects these parents and their wonderful skills.

One note of caution: We focus here on challenging but primarily routine situations that can usually be addressed within the sphere of family and school. If your child is not responding to your best efforts, please do not give up. There is wonderful assistance available to you. Try your child's teacher and the school counselor or social worker. Perhaps your doctor can help or a professional trained in dealing with youth and family issues. Especially be alert for the more serious problems of alcohol, marijuana, and other drug use, depression, eating disorders, problems with anger and violence, hyperactivity, and attention deficit disorder. There are new and exciting ways we can help our children live wonderful lives. Do not give up.

Speaking of not giving up, this revision of *What to Say or Do* would not have been possible without the hard work and good humor of Bette Nowacki and Nancy Campbell. Each of us made the others' work stronger and clearer. David Wilmes made invaluable contributions to the final draft.

We salute your caring and nurturing instinct, your willingness to reach out to your child in what sometimes can be confusing, frustrating, and painful times. Use this book. Try out new things, and love and laugh along the way. Feel free to investigate Hazelden's other family resources—books, pamphlets, videos, and our Web site—and perhaps even attend a parent training session. We would love to have you at *Roots & Wings!*

May parenting bring you new ways to live and love.

SECTION CONTENTS

section

① ages 2-4

Example Behaviors

- Your two-year-old son won't let other children touch his toys.

- Your toddler refuses to share food, such as giving one of her cookies to another child.

- Your child is overly possessive about her favorite belongings and cries and hits if her sister tries to use or play with them.

Thinking about It...

Toddlers naturally have a hard time sharing. They're just getting used to having an identity separate from their parents. At the same time, they're coming to know that certain objects are theirs. Their attachments to these objects can be strong. For example, when a child sees a parent simply looking at his new red toy truck, the child may grab the truck, clutch it to his chest, and loudly rebuke, "*Mine!*" Later, when parents begin urging a child to share, the child will likely protest even more. For the toddler, sharing seems like the very opposite of what should be going on with *his* prized possessions!

What to Say or Do

1. Model generosity by sharing often with your child, other adults, and other children. Call your child's attention to what you are doing: "Daddy's going to share his fishing rod with Uncle LeRoy." "Here, Cassie, I'll share my apple slices with you."

2. Avoid forcing your child to share. It's normal for young children to have difficulty sharing. Notice how very young children play side-by-side but not *with* each other. Learning to share develops gradually and cannot be rushed. At first, simply focus on creating a generous and fair environment.

3. Talk to your child about the value of sharing. Say, for example, "When you share your things, others will enjoy playing with you!"

4. Begin teaching your child whatever rules you will have for sharing. Some examples of simple sharing rules: "If you put a toy down, anyone may play with it. If you have it in your hands, you may keep it." "Each person can only play with one toy at a time."

5. Allow your child to choose two or three favorite objects (his blanket, the blue ball) that needn't be shared and several others that he's willing to share. Giving your child a feeling of control over the belongings he cares about most will help him to consider sharing. Even so, be ready to supervise the many situations that will call for sharing.

6. Sometimes safety issues arise when your toddler fights with another child over a toy or an object. When this happens, take the toy away, saying, "I'm afraid you might hit each other with this toy, and that would hurt! Now, let's see... what's something different that you two friends could do?" If needed, encourage them to look for two other toys to play with.

7. Make up some sharing games to play within your family. Even simple games, such as asking your child to share a pile of crayons or blocks by giving one to each person in the room, will give her practice in how sharing works and feels.

8. Encourage your toddler's friends to bring a toy or game when coming over to play. If they seem to want to play with each other's toys, help them share by taking turns.

9. Show your older toddler that your family values sharing by letting him accompany you when donating and delivering books, clothes, or food to charities. Explain that you are sharing because not everyone has enough books, clothes, or food. Doing this will help increase your child's sense of abundance and concern for others.

10. Designate certain objects such as food, the TV, and certain books and games in your home as "shared" property. This will help your child get used to the concept of sharing.

11. Acknowledge your child's behavior when she starts to share. Use casual verbal reinforcement such as, "I see you're sharing your markers with Ricardo!" Or give your child a gentle pat while saying, "Nice sharing!" Stating your comments casually, in a matter-of-fact tone lets your child know that the behavior is expected.

Resolve

I value generosity and fair play. I resolve to work patiently to help my child learn how to share and to respect other people's rights to their possessions.

SMART TIP

When your toddler is generous, take some time to talk with him about how good it feels to share. Help your child discover and express his feelings of satisfaction and pride.

Example Behaviors

• Your daughter whines when she doesn't get what she wants.

• Your toddler whines to get attention.

• Your three-year-old son whines when he can't find anything to do.

Thinking about It...

Whining is a seemingly endless stream of monotonous pleading or nagging, voiced in a high-pitched, nasal tone. A child's whining usually begins around age two and a half and tapers off around age four, peaking at about age three and a half. If not addressed, whining can become a habit that continues into the school years—and adulthood! Most whining starts out when a child wants attention, wants his or her own way, or is simply tired or cranky. Some children try out whining just as they try out speaking slowly, rapidly, loudly, and softly, or with high and low tones. When parents give in to persistent whining, the child learns that whining gets results.

What to Say or Do

1. Be sure to spend some undivided time with your child every day. Put your other affairs aside, turn off the TV, and give him your attention. Whether you play together, act silly, talk (ask him questions to get him going), or take a walk, be sure you are tuned in to him, his needs, and his talents.

2. Keep your child busy. A toddler cannot be expected to fill her day constructively without some guidance. Think ahead, keeping her current interests in mind. Sometimes all that's needed is a suggestion. You might, for example, suggest a new twist, perhaps a pretend situation, for playing with an old toy.

3. Be responsive. When your preschooler speaks to you without whining, answer as soon as possible. Preface your answer with an acknowledgment of what he said, for example: "Oh, it sounds as if you're hungry..." or "Yes, I know it's hard...."

4. If you can't respond right away when your child speaks to you, signal or say that you hear him. Quickly free up yourself and thank him for waiting.

5. Use role play to show the difference between whining and speaking normally. Or record your child's whining. Later, when her whining is over and she is calm, play the tape for her. Being careful not to mock, identify her way of speaking as whining, and then help her practice saying the words without whining. Once you're sure she knows what whining is, make it clear that you don't like whining and will not respond to it.

6. Avoid making too many exceptions to your other household rules. If your child knows he can't watch TV during certain hours, he will be less apt to whine for it.

7. Acknowledge your child's anger, frustration, or disappointment but not her whining by saying, "I want to hear about your problem when you're ready to use your nice voice," or "It's much easier to hear about your feelings when you don't whine."

8. When your older toddler whines, remind him to use a normal tone of voice, or say, "Please ask your question with your normal voice, and I'll be happy to answer." If the whining continues, ignore the request and move a noticeable distance away.

9. No matter how much your child's whining escalates, resist the urge to stop it by giving in to her demands. Instead, say, "I think we need a little break." Ask her to pick a spot where she can settle down. Tell her that when she feels that she can talk about what she wants in a nice way without whining, she can come back to you to talk about it. Keep in mind that it is important for your child to feel some control as she learns to behave responsibly.

10. After your toddler knows the tone of voice you expect, be sure to acknowledge him when he uses that tone. Say, "I like the way you asked me that, Cory."

11. Even when you think you have your child's whining under control, be ready for it to crop up again from time to time, such as when she is overly tired.

Resolve

I value clear communication, and I resolve to help my child learn to replace her whining with more direct and pleasantly spoken requests and comments.

SMART TIP

Remember not to whine yourself. A parent's complaining can sound like whining to a child. If you catch yourself drawing out comments like, *"Geez, why* can't Lucy drive us to the meeting?" or "Oh, *now* I suppose I'll have to do it all over again!" work toward eliminating the tone of complaint.

3

WON'T EAT THE WAY YOU WANT HER TO EAT

Example Behaviors

- Your daughter will only eat macaroni and cheese.
- Your child dawdles over his food, eating and not eating.
- Your toddler refuses to eat vegetables.

Thinking about It...

Preschool children are typically uninterested in food at meal-times. Their appetite drops off noticeably after their first two years of exceptional growth. The parent who is trying to offer a balanced meal is puzzled, frustrated, and often worried. Why is his child eating so little? It helps to put food, or nourishment, in perspective. Even though she may skip entire meals, the healthy preschool child will get a balanced diet over several days of eating. Her appetite will pick up again when she needs it during the early school years.

What to Say or Do

1. Put small portions on your child's plate, cut into bite-size pieces, and try to include at least one food you know she likes. Be prepared, however. Preschoolers' tastes change rapidly—what she liked last week may be refused when offered again.

2. Establish regular times to eat even though your preschooler's appetite fluctuates. His body will gradually learn a three-meals-per-day rhythm. Offer a variety of healthy foods at those mealtimes.

3. Be sure to offer healthy snacks to your child. Preschoolers *need* a nutritious snack in midmorning and midafternoon. They may eat less than you might expect at mealtimes, but they need to eat more often. Set out several nonsugary foods, such as raisins, carrots, whole wheat crackers, apple slices

with peanut butter, and so on. Let your child choose which snack she wants. (Convenient but sugar-laden snacks—such as candy, cookies, soft drinks, and many cereals—can lead to cavities. Being relatively high in calories and low in nutrition, such snacks also contribute to excessive weight gain.)

4. Allow your younger toddler to feed himself, assisting only as needed. His awkward (and sometimes messy!) first attempts to feed himself soon will become more coordinated.

5. Keep mealtimes pleasant. Focus on conversation and not on how much your child is eating. Let her decide which foods to try and how much to eat. Let her eat at her own pace. If she's not eating, relax and remember your child will probably not eat much at any one meal.

6. Be alert for cues that your child is no longer hungry. Some playing with food occurs as part of your toddler's need to explore, but absently stirring or playing with food, squirming, whining, and so on indicate lack of hunger. When such behavior starts, ask her if she's done. If she's not sure, say, "Tell me when you're finished, and I'll take your plate." If she continues not eating, follow through, matter-of-factly taking her plate. As you learn to recognize her varying appetite, respect it and let that overcome any traces of exasperation or worry you might have. It is important that she not be required to "clean her plate."

7. Strive to make mealtime fun. Involve your child in helping with the preparations, such as making out a grocery list, shopping for the food, setting the table, and cooking. Be sure to have a few laughs during mealtime.

8. If you have a picky eater or a child on a "food jag" (he'll only eat cereal, for example), avoid trying to control his eating. These behaviors are normal. Simply continue to offer a wide range of healthy meals and snacks and allow your child to eat whatever he chooses from that food.

Resolve

I resolve to offer my child nutritious meals and snacks and to respect and trust my child's appetite, letting her choose what she will eat and how much.

SMART TIP Offer a few food choices to help your child feel in control. Say, "Do you want carrots or green beans tonight?" "Would you like white or chocolate milk?" "Do you want your sandwich plain or toasted?"

Example Behaviors

• Your three-year-old hits, kicks, bites, or scratches other kids.

• Your child plays rough on the preschool playground.

• Your daughter hits you or throws objects at you.

Thinking about It...

Toddlers who hit, kick, throw things, bite, or scratch usually do not *intend* to physically hurt someone. At times, they might simply be riding out a building momentum of energy that surprises even them. Other times, it could be an outburst of pent-up frustration or anger. Often, they are trying to control a situation, such as keeping possession of a favorite toy. Or maybe they were encouraged to hurl a ball as far as they could in the backyard that morning—why not do the same with the shiny metal dump truck? Whatever the reason, these behaviors, which can result in damage to property and hurting others, call for prompt intervention.

What to Say or Do

1. When your child behaves aggressively, immediately restrain her from continuing. Then state simple, clear rules for appropriate behavior. For example, "We don't hurt other people. We try to get along." "Let's be kind and gentle with each other." "Oops, we don't throw things inside the house." Explain to your child that hitting hurts others, and it's important to respect other people and not hurt them.

2. Be gentle in your own behavior. Your aggressive behavior shows your child how to be aggressive when he is angry.

3. Closely supervise your toddler's play. Intervene at once if he causes physical harm. Remove your child from the situation. Ask, "How would you feel if that happened to you?" "How do you think Robby feels?" If aggressive behavior occurs several times, you might say, "You won't be able to play anymore until you've calmed down."

4. Cultivate your child's gentle interactions with living things, such as your family pet, or a bird, squirrel, or butterfly. For example, help your child watch wild creatures quietly and not scare them. Teach your child how to talk to and gently pet your cat, dog, or other pet. You might help your child put a soft blanket or small stuffed animal beside your dozing, curled-up cat, saying, "Here you go, Sasha. Have a nice, little sleep!"

5. Try some role playing with your toddler about treating each other kindly. For instance, you might have a stuffed bunny pounce on a small teddy bear. Then have another stuffed animal say, "Oh, dear! Please don't hurt my friend Baby Bear. We all play together around here." Then have the bunny nuzzle the bear, saying, "I'm sorry, Baby Bear. I hope you're OK. Let's play!"

6. Help your child know what to do besides hit or throw objects. Encourage him to ask a grown-up for help. Give frequent reminders about asking for help.

7. Help your older toddler talk about how she feels when she behaves aggressively. Let her know that being upset and feeling mad or angry happens sometimes, and that it can happen suddenly. Naming feelings and talking about them can lessen some of their power.

8. Name and briefly describe your own feelings as you go about your day. For instance, "Oh, dear, we didn't get any mail. I'm disappointed we didn't get any mail from Aunt Louisa. I feel a little sad." Hearing your feelings in context helps your child understand their meaning.

9. If your toddler is hitting you, firmly restrain him and say, "No, you may not hit Mommy. That hurt. Let's think about what else we can do besides hitting."

10. At times, restraint may be needed, but *do not hurt your child* to stop his hitting or kicking. Even though your child may be behaving quite aggressively, use of painful physical force to "teach him a lesson" is never OK.

11. Acknowledge your child when she is upset and behaves without being aggressive. You might say, "You can be very proud of yourself. You were mad and you talked about it instead of hurting others."

Resolve

*I resolve to teach my child appropriate
alternatives to aggressive behavior.*

SMART TIP

Encourage your child to say "I'm sorry" if she hurts another child. This is an effective way of teaching your child to take responsibility for her actions. Be careful to not force this, however. She will apologize when she can.

Example Behaviors

- Your toddler keeps getting out of bed after you've tucked him in.

- Your child keeps asking for more bedtime stories, or for water or hugs.

- Your three-year-old cries and won't go to sleep without you beside her in bed or in a nearby chair.

Thinking about It...

Getting enough sleep is vital, especially during the growing years. Getting enough sleep helps a child stay healthy, grow and have energy, and be more alert the next day. Yet toddlers resist bedtime for many reasons: It's not fun, they might miss something, they want to continue being near you, or resisting bedtime has gone on for so long that it's become habitual.

What to Say or Do

1. Strive to make going to bed a special time. Occasionally, in the daytime, make casual positive references to your child's bed or bedtime accessories: "There's your cozy bed and your nighttime friends [stuffed animal, toy, special pillow, blanket]!" In the early evening, you might say, "Soon we can have our story time, snuggling in the covers!" or "Mm-m, a little later we can get in our comfy beds!" Don't look for any agreement or response from your child. Matter-of-fact, no-strings comments like these can pique a child's interest and set up an attraction to the activity.

2. Decide on a definite lights-out time, and keep it consistent. Except for special occasions, stick to it.

3. Avoid rushing your child to bed because it's "suddenly" bedtime. Children resist being rushed from one thing to

another. Use the hour before the actual lights-out time as a quieting, gentle transition between his long day and rest. Give your child your full and soothing attention. Accepting that such a peaceful transition takes about an hour will help you enjoy it yourself, without being hurried or tense.

4. Create and follow a consistent bedtime sequence. When the order of the bedtime routine is unpredictable, a child may feel off balance, not really sure if going to bed will be carried out in full. The nightly sequence might include some or all of the following: bathing, brushing teeth, putting on pajamas, reading stories or telling made-up ones, singing lullabies, cuddling or backrubs, having a drink of water, saying a prayer—even checking for monsters under the bed. (Ask baby-sitters to follow the same schedule and sequence.)

5. During the story or cuddle time, hugging your child and saying, "Mm-m, this is nice!" or "I like our time together at bedtime!" is another way of helping him connect bedtime with a pleasant time.

6. With an older toddler, you might lie down with your child or sit in her room for ten or fifteen minutes, talking about what she did and saw that day and then something she can look forward to the next day. Having a nightlight on in your child's room or adjacent hallway can help her feel safe and secure.

7. If your child is clearly not sleepy after the quieting hour before lights-out, let him stay up in his bed. Allow him to have a few toys and invite him to use his imagination

to figure out some quiet play. After about fifteen minutes, come in to say goodnight and turn the lights out.

8. If your child gets out of bed, attend to what she needs and then tuck her in again. If she gets up again, say only, "Go back to your bed, please." (Escort the very young child.) If your child comes into your bedroom, let her know that your bedroom is your sleeping area, not hers, and bring her back to her own place for sleep.

9. Avoid letting your child's afternoon nap slip into the later hours of the day.

10. If your child is brimming with energy after dinner, do some physical activity (playing catch, tumbling, jumping rope) with him in the early evening.

11. If an exhausting struggle about bedtime has been occurring each night with your child, gaining control may take more time. Remember your resolve and your reasons behind it. With calmness, patience, and firmness, clearly explain the new limits and start incorporating the above suggestions.

Resolve

I resolve to care for my child's health and to continue to establish my role as parent by setting and maintaining appropriate bedtime rules.

SMART TIP

Some elaborately drawn-out, repetitive stories and counting books do wonders in bringing on sleep. Find and reserve a few of these for those nights when your child is wide awake.

Example Behaviors

- Your child demands your attention when you're talking to someone else by poking or tugging at you.

- Your four-year-old persistently interrupts you when you're on the telephone.

- Your daughter won't let you finish a sentence without breaking in.

Thinking about It...

The very nature of a parent-child relationship means the child receives an enormous amount of attention and supervision from the parent. Young children come to expect this kind of attention. When a parent is busy speaking animatedly with another adult or is speaking on the telephone, a child might wonder why things are changing or even feel slightly abandoned. The child interrupts the parent to regain the attention he's so used to. If one interruption fails to stop the parent's conversation, the child can become increasingly insistent, including poking and pulling and loud cries of "Mommy! Mommy!" These normal reactions of children can be embarrassing for parents. This situation naturally leads to helping your child learn to wait his turn and to be considerate of others.

What to Say or Do

1. Letting your child know what's going to happen is an effective way to cut down on interruptions. You might say, for example, "In a few minutes, a man named Mr. Sato is coming to see Daddy. I'll be asking Mr. Sato some questions, and I'll be writing on some papers. I want you to be with us, and I need you to play quietly so we can get our work done quickly. Let's pick out some of your

favorite puzzles or quiet toys that you can play with while Mr. Sato is here.'"

2. Set an example by not interrupting your child or other family members, unless the matter is quite important. When you must interrupt, be sure to say "excuse me" or "I'm sorry to interrupt, but..."

3. Take opportunities to point out to your toddler when you are waiting to speak with someone else. For example, as you are second in line to return some merchandise, tell your child that you need to talk to the person behind the counter, but you are waiting until he is finished speaking with the person in front of you.

4. Explain to your child that when you are on the telephone or speaking with someone in person, she will need to wait to talk to you until you are finished. As she is learning and forgets the rule, put your finger to your lips and say a gentle "sh-hh," reminding her to wait.

5. Try to limit the length of your conversations during the period when your child is learning how to wait. The younger your child is, of course, the less time he or she can wait. If you know a telephone call is going to take five or ten minutes, try placing a free-standing timer where your child can see it. Set it for the time you expect to be busy and tell your child you will be free at about the same time the pointer moves to zero and the timer rings.

6. When you anticipate being occupied in conversation, remove from your younger toddler's sight any objects that usually need your supervision (such as finger paints, Magic Markers, bubbles, and Play-Doh). Then involve your child in an absorbing activity such as building with blocks or playing with stuffed animals or plastic containers.

7. Create a special box of "waiting toys" that your child can play with during the times she'll need to wait while you are on the phone. Similarly, take along a few toys when you and your child go places where you'll be engaged in conversation with others.

8. Thank your child when she waits instead of interrupting, saying, "Thank you so much for waiting while I was busy with Carlos."

9. Teach your child about taking turns to talk. Make it a game, using a stopwatch or a timer, in which your child and then you each get to say anything you want for thirty seconds without interruption. Continue for about two or three rounds, saying, "Now it's your [or my] turn to talk!" after each thirty-second period.

10. Sometimes your toddler just can't wait. If you sense one of these times, you may want to excuse yourself briefly from your conversation, come to your child's eye level, and give him your attention in a relaxed way. Doing this is often a relatively quick way to satisfy his need and return to your conversation with no more interruptions.

Resolve

I resolve to teach my child how to wait
her turn and to be considerate of others.

SMART TIP

Before beginning an adult conversation, ask your toddler how she is doing or if she needs to talk to you about anything. Meeting your child's needs will help you feel comfortable when asking her to wait.

Example Behaviors

• Your son kicks and screams when you're trying to get him dressed.

• Your child gets hysterical when she doesn't get her way.

• Your toddler has a fit in a public place (park, shopping mall, grocery store, and so on).

Thinking about It...

Temper tantrums are a period of intense crying, yelling, trembling, shaking, or flailing about to express anger or frustration. Temper tantrums are common in the toddler years. Parents usually patiently "wait out" a tantrum. The tantrums of a toddler can be upsetting, frustrating, and frightening to a parent. Fortunately, tantrums usually cease before the school years begin. Parents can hasten their fading away by teaching their child that it's OK to be angry, but there are better ways to express this emotion.

What to Say or Do

1. When your child begins to throw a tantrum, remain calm and say, "I can't talk to you when you scream and kick. When you stop, we can talk." Move some distance away and do not try to reason or talk your child out of the tantrum *during* the tantrum. Attention only encourages the tantrum.

2. Get to know your child's needs and preferences to help avoid tantrums. Notice cues that indicate what he likes and doesn't like. As you spend time playing and being with your child, be supportive and encouraging. A child who feels his parent is a trusted ally is less likely to become highly frustrated.

3. Model peaceful behavior. When you're frustrated or angry, avoid yelling and pounding furniture. Children mimic the behavior of the adults in their lives. Keep things in perspective though, and avoid feeling guilty if you aren't always calm and collected. We all raise our voices and get somewhat agitated at times.

4. Prepare your child for coming events. Children need to be informed about what's going to happen next. When you take time to describe coming activities, your child feels included and can let go of fear or anxiety that comes with not knowing. You might say, for example, "Now we're going to get in the car to go to a store. We're going to have our pictures taken. We want a picture of you and Daddy and Mommy all together. Then we want a special picture of just you. We'll all need to sit very still to help the pictures turn out nicely." Depending on your situation, you might add, "Which small toy would you like to bring to be in the pictures with you?"

5. Limit trips to grocery stores, malls, and other places that can be overstimulating to a child who habitually throws tantrums in public.

6. At a time when your child is relaxed, use role play—perhaps using dolls, stuffed animals, or puppets—to teach your child how to express anger and to ask for help for what she wants. Encourage her to use "feelings" and "want" words, such as, "I'm *mad* that I have to go to sleep!" or "You won't buy me that toy, and I'm *mad*."

"I *want* this tower to stay up! Please *help me*."

7. Offer your toddler a substantial, nutritious snack in midmorning and in midafternoon. Late morning or late afternoon tantrums are sometimes brought on by hunger. You might, for example, serve your child a half sandwich, some fruit and cheese, or a cup of hearty soup or chili.

8. Identify other conditions that might be triggering your child's tantrums. For instance, if you notice your child is usually tired when tantrums come on, pay special attention to her getting enough sleep. If tantrums happen more in the hottest part of the summer, see that she has frequent cool drinks and sits in the shade as needed.

9. Acknowledge your child's feelings. You might say, "I know you're angry right now," or "I'd be mad too, if..."

10. If your child throws tantrums, be sure to acknowledge him when he manages to avoid that behavior. Say, for example, "I'm happy to help you when you ask so nicely for what you want," or, with the older toddler, "Good for you! You should be proud of yourself for handling your anger so well."

11. Remember, throwing tantrums is normal, especially for young children who have fewer language skills. A tantrum is a sign of the child's frustration and not a sign that you are a bad parent.

Resolve

I resolve to help my child begin to build a healthy emotional life by teaching her to identify her emotions of frustration, disappointment, and anger and to express them productively.

SMART TIP

When your child is having a tantrum in public—such as in a toy store, at a movie, in a restaurant—simply remove him from the situation. Even if it's raining or snowing, grab your coats, take him outside, and wait until he calms down.

SECTION CONTENTS

section ② ages 5–7

Example Behaviors

• Your five-year-old often forgets to brush his teeth.

• Your daughter usually forgets to do her chores.

• Your child often drops all his school things by the door.

Thinking about It...

Remembering routine tasks and behaviors takes time with many children ages five to seven. At home, these children can be keenly absorbed in their own play and activities. At the same time, their curiosity easily moves them from one activity to another. During the school year, children take in huge amounts of new information in their kindergarten, first-, and second-grade classrooms. Children these ages often need reminders to keep them on track about tasks and behaviors desired by the parent. A parent's positive attitude that self-discipline will eventually take hold is valuable during these times.

What to Say or Do

1. Keep directions for each task or behavior simple and clear. Think a minute about the best way to word such a direction before giving it.

2. When you need to repeat a direction for a task, try to use the same words you used the first time you gave it. Doing so helps your child remember the direction and also helps her know your expectation is firm and consistent.

3. Make eye contact with your child when giving directions for a task or behavior to make sure you have his attention.

4. Explain to your child more of the reason for doing the routine task or behavior than you may have when he was younger. For example, "Little bits of food that stay on

your teeth cause holes, or cavities, in the teeth. As these holes grow larger, your teeth may hurt. Brushing every day gets rid of the food so the holes can't start. Then you'll have strong teeth that don't hurt."

5. At times, especially when your child is tired or just learning a new task, you may want to do a task *with* your child, but avoid doing it *for* him. Be sure your child is participating alongside you.

6. Do some tasks or behaviors as a family. For example, when the whole family gets into the car, you might say, "Safety check! Time to fasten seat belts!" before starting the engine. Children who feel a sense of belonging and shared goals have an easier time remembering the task or behavior on their own.

7. Whenever possible, space out the tasks you expect your child to do over the day. Remembering to follow through on expected tasks takes energy. When too many tasks cluster together, kids often falter.

8. Occasionally shift assignments for routine household chores. If your child begins to slack off on folding part of the laundry, give her a choice of doing one of two alternatives—perhaps feeding the dog or emptying wastebaskets.

9. Add humor, such as making up a silly song to doing some routine tasks. For example, have some fun by marching with your child into the bathroom, singing, *"Holy moly, no! We don't want holey teeth!"* (Sing in a jaunty, march-like tune, stressing every other syllable.)

10. Give your reminders with an encouraging (not exasperated!) tone.

11. As your child's self-discipline improves, turn some of the reminding over to the child. For instance, you might ask him to help you make a list of the daily tasks he's expected to do. Each time he completes a task without your reminder, he can put a happy face next to it. Once a week, review the list and faces together and discuss his progress.

12. Acknowledge your child when he does follow through without reminders. Even a simple nod and "Nice job!" goes a long way.

Resolve

I resolve to support my child as she learns to do routine tasks and behaviors—relating to health, safety, and the home—on her own, with fewer prompts.

SMART TIP   When a task needs to be done immediately, firmly insist that your child do so. Avoid allowing your child to buy time in doing the task. It's easy to get hooked into his "I'll do it in a minute," which sometimes turns into ten minutes, an hour, or never. The simplest, most effective reaction is a consistent "We need to do this now."

Example Behaviors

• Your daughter gets into the medicine cabinet.

• Your child plays with matches, knives, or power tools.

• Your five-year-old son gets into a jug of bleach.

Thinking about It...

Parents want to nurture, not squelch, a child's tremendous curiosity and instinct to explore the surrounding environment. When a child's curiosity leads to exploring danger zones, however, immediate intervention and education are vital. Without first- or secondhand experience or education, a child has no knowledge of the many objects and situations that are potential hazards to his or her safety.

What to Say or Do

1. Eliminate as much risk as possible by putting dangerous items like guns, power tools, and poisons in a locked cabinet or other place that is impossible for your child to get into.

2. Do not leave any dangerous items lying around the house, porches, basement, garage, or yard. For example, put matches, knives, large scissors, and household chemical agents away immediately after using them. Find secure places for handsaws, sheets of glass, nails, gasoline, turpentine, and so on.

3. Choose childproof caps for all medications and purchase childproof lighters.

4. Have several talks with your child about the dangerous items that are off-limits. Let her see the items and ask questions about them. Avoid saying only that something is "dangerous." Be sure your child understands the reason each item is dangerous. Include dangerous situations, like what causes electrical shock.

5. Be fairly explicit with your child about the serious consequences of getting into the things that are off-limits. For instance, you might say, "If you cut yourself with a knife, it will hurt and you'll bleed." "If you swallow these dangerous liquids, you'll become very sick and have to go to the hospital."

6. Make a habit of putting a neon-colored "Do NOT touch" or "STOP" sticker on off-limits items—such as bleach and other strong cleaners, lighter fluid, and sprays with hazardous ingredients—as you buy them. Let your child know he should not touch these items.

7. Caution your child to be just as careful about dangerous things she might see at neighbors' or friends' houses, along alleys, near garbage cans, and elsewhere.

8. Incorporate some fun in teaching your child about dangerous, off-limits items. For example, let your child present a pretend TV commercial explaining why kids should stay away from matches, tools, knives, and other dangerous things. Doing this will help you check your child's knowledge as well as reinforce the dangers to her.

9. Give your child safe substitutes to play
'with, such as age-appropriate toolboxes
or children's doctor's kits.

10. Acknowledge your child when he
deliberately chooses to avoid touching
or playing with dangerous objects.
Say, "I see that you know what can
hurt you."

Resolve

*I resolve to take every precaution to childproof our
home and to educate my child about the consequences
of getting into dangerous objects and situations.*

**SMART
TIP**

Teach your child to call 911 and the local
poison control center (put the numbers on
your telephones) in case of an emergency.
Despite your best efforts, your child may
intentionally or accidentally get into
something dangerous. Have contingency
plans in place.

DOESN'T TAKE CARE OF BELONGINGS

Example Behaviors

- Your child leaves her bike near the alley overnight.
- Your first-grader plays in mud while wearing his new school shoes.
- Your daughter doodles with markers in her schoolbooks.

Thinking about It...

Some children naturally take fairly good care of their belongings. Others do not. They may not be aware of the value of their belongings, have no thoughts about the consequences of their careless actions, be preoccupied and not realize what they are doing, and so on. A large part of correcting careless behavior with possessions is raising awareness.

What to Say or Do

1. Show your child how her special objects are to be treated. If, for example, she gets a new bike, show her how to use the kickstand and horn, how to lock the bike, how to wash it, and where to store it overnight. Also, explain how the tires work and why to avoid riding over sharp objects, like broken glass.

2. Create an orderly environment in which there are practical and specific places where your child's belongings should be kept.

3. Set an example by taking good care of your own belongings. If your child happens to be present, explain what you are doing and why. You might say, for example, "I'm cleaning these paintbrushes really well, so they won't be too stiff when they dry. I need to use them again next week," or "Well, I guess I can't wear my white shoes. It's starting to rain and I don't want them ruined."

4. Explain to your child why it's important to care for belongings. For example, you might say, "Having one special place to put things [books, games, watercolors, and so on] helps you know exactly where to find them when you want them," or "Your new school shoes cost a fair amount of money, and they need to be kept clean and dry so they will last."

5. Help your child think through where certain items belong: "Where do you think the best place is to put your socks when they are dirty?" "Amanda, let's pick out a safe place to put your new glasses each night before bed."

6. When the care of an item is relatively simple, involve your child in making a plan for its care: "Let's see, how can we keep the play money in this game from getting lost or wrinkled up?"

7. Have your child save up to buy (or help to buy) something he wants, such as a kite or yo-yo. When he does extra chores or saves from his allowance for this item, your child will gain a sense of ownership, begin to understand the value of money, and be likely to take care of the purchase.

8. Encourage your child to choose a special toy or other belonging to bring to school for show-and-tell. Sharing a favorite possession highlights its importance and may help her want to take good care of it.

9. If something you are purchasing for your child involves special care or handling, such as some goldfish, stress the overall care to him before the purchase. After the purchase, be sure your child understands the importance of each aspect of the needed care and the consequences of failing to practice that care.

10. Casually acknowledge your child when she puts her things in their designated places and when she gives certain items the care they need. For example, "Hey, you're smart, putting all those caps back on! Those markers aren't going to dry out on you!" "Hey, you're keeping those sneakers really clean!"

Resolve

I resolve to teach my child to understand the value of her belongings and to care for them.

SMART TIP

If your child habitually loses items or does not keep items in reasonably good condition, let him go without the item or help pay for its replacement.

Example Behaviors

- Your son argues when you say he can't do something.

- Your child keeps pushing and pushing, hoping to wear you down until you give in to whatever she wants.

- Your six-year-old keeps saying, "It's not fair!"

Thinking about It...

Most children ages five to seven occasionally slip into complaining, arguing, and even accusing injustice when they are denied something they want. Children's opposing behaviors increase, however, when a parent unintentionally reinforces them. For example, a parent who is distracted, tired, or stressed-out may give up and *give in* to a child's barrage, letting the child have her own way just to end the pestering. The parent is relieved the pushing and arguing are over. The child, however, has learned that if she argues long enough she can reverse her parent's "no."

What to Say or Do

1. Avoid saying no to trivial things that really don't matter. Some parents say no when it's not necessary, thinking it's an opportunity to teach their child to "behave" or "mind them." But doing so has the opposite effect. The child will sense injustice and see the parent as overly restrictive.

2. Decide what is and isn't negotiable. For example, you might be willing to compromise somewhat on how much TV your child can watch on the weekend, but are firm in your convictions about what sort of programming you consider appropriate.

3. When setting a limit, be sure to give a simple explanation for it. For example, "You can't have any chips now so close to dinnertime, because they will spoil your appetite."

4. Do not listen or attend to your child if she is relating to you in a manipulative, rude, or disrespectful way. Your attention encourages the child to continue in that way.

5. If your child argues in a respectful way, hear him out. If there's no new information that causes you to change your mind, you might say, "I understand how you feel, but the answer is still no."

6. Acknowledge your child's feelings of anger and disappointment. Say, for example, "I can see that you feel angry [or disappointed]. Mom and I have these feelings sometimes, too—like yesterday, when we learned we couldn't go to Florida. Sometimes we just have to say, 'OK, I guess I can't have what I want.'"

7. If a situation comes up and you're not sure where you stand, tell your child you'll think about it so that you aren't responding under pressure. Be sure to give her your response, though, as soon as possible.

8. Teach your child how to express dissent. For example, encourage her to practice saying, "I know your reason, but I still want it," or "Well, all right, but I feel mad about this."

9. Acknowledge your child when he does not continue to argue with you. "I really appreciate it, Ravi, when you accept and respect my decision."

Resolve

To help my child respect my decisions,
I resolve to be sure I mean no before
I say it and—unless new information
changes my mind—to stick to that decision.

SMART TIP

To help you not give in to your child's resistance, keep your stress level to a minimum. Be sure you are getting adequate sleep, nutrition, exercise, and positive contact with others.

Example Behaviors

- Your child swears or makes obscene gestures.

- Your daughter speaks rudely to some guests at your home.

- Your seven-year-old son cuts in line.

Thinking about It...

By around age five, young children are becoming more aware of the many types of manners used in interactions with others. These young children encounter mixed messages about manners daily. What they are learning at home about manners doesn't always match what they see in the manners of some of their peers, on TV shows, in movies and videos, or in various public places. Parents sometimes need to guide children in sorting out what's appropriate.

What to Say or Do

1. Increase or even exaggerate the frequency of your own verbal manners—such as saying please, thank you, excuse me, pardon me, may I help you—during the time your child is learning to make good manners a habit.

2. Talk with your child if she is making rude remarks to others. Sometimes a child doesn't realize that what she is doing is impolite. Open the conversation to a broader discussion of manners in general. You might ask, "What other times are you not sure what to do?" or "What other manners seem puzzling to you?"

3. Use the manners you want your child to use, at home and elsewhere. Being around a consistently well-mannered parent is one of the best ways a child can learn good manners.

4. State rules for good manners in a positive way. Rather than telling your child what *not* to do, say, for example, "Stand at the end of the line and wait your turn," or "Please talk, Emmie, after you're done swallowing your food."

5. Watch for rude behavior of others that will help you explain good manners to your child. For example, when swearing occurs on TV, talk to your child about those words and any other language that is impolite and should not be used.

6. Expect respect and politeness from your child and prompt it. Verbal nudges that do not tell your child exactly what to say—such as, "What would you like to say to Aunt Martina for having such a nice birthday party for you?"—can instill confidence.

7. Teach your child that having good manners is one of the most basic and important ways to show respect for others. It is also a way to respect himself, for when he uses good manners it shows others he expects them to treat him politely as well.

8. Acknowledge your child when he uses good manners without a reminder. For example, you might say, "I liked the way you held the door open for the boy on crutches."

9. Avoid correcting your child in front of others. Take him aside and talk about the situation in private.

10. Encourage your child to apologize as soon as possible for her disrespectful behavior. If she seems embarrassed to do this verbally, she may want to write a note of apology.

Resolve

I resolve to teach my child to use good manners and to expect them from others.

SMART TIP

When your child's manners need correction, be careful to communicate that it's her *behavior*, not her, that is the problem.

Example Behaviors

• Your daughter frequently teases small children until they cry.

• Your child scares other kids and starts fights in the neighborhood and at school.

• Your six-year-old son is verbally threatening or abusive to others.

Thinking about It...

Children bully others for various reasons. A child may simply want something, such as candy, that another child has. Research indicates that children who bully aren't aware of how their behavior affects others. Others have been bullied themselves and are trying it out. Some children resort to bullying when they are unsure about how to interact in a new situation. Bullying is a serious problem behavior that needs to be curtailed at its first sign.

What to Say or Do

1. Discuss your child's behavior if she frequently teases others or is overly aggressive. Talk to her about what's OK and what is off-limits. Help her distinguish between teasing that is harmless and teasing that goes too far. You might say, "Teasing Janna once about her messy ice cream face is fine. Teasing her over and over about her freckles is not."

2. Play "be the leader" with your child to help him learn about alternatives to his aggressive behavior. First, take turns being a bossy, aggressive leader (the leader could be organizing a game) while the other is afraid of the leader and having a hard time following along. Then, take turns being a helpful leader with the other learning easily and following along with more enjoyment. After the role

plays, talk about what your child thinks about being each kind of leader. (Examples of leader situations: teaching how to throw a ball, how to do a somersault, how to play a game.)

3. Talk with your child about how her behavior affects others. Discuss positive and negative reactions to her behavior. Helping children understand the impact they have on others increases their sense of empathy.

4. Ask your child to think about how the characters might feel when you read to him or watch a TV show with him.

5. Talk to your child's teachers. Let them know you are working with your child to correct his aggressive behavior and ask for their observations and suggestions. Discuss the possibility of the teacher giving your child a leadership role occasionally to help him feel pride in that responsibility.

6. Supervise your child's play with others in your home and yard. Observe what seems to set off her aggressive behavior. Look for patterns. Is she cranky before she gets aggressive? Do others provoke her? Does she seem to have problems getting along with all children or a specific few? Answers to these questions will help you move in the right direction to improve the behavior.

7. Think about whether your child is feeling inferior in any way. Sometimes mean, bossy, or rough behavior is a cover-up for feelings of insecurity or fear of being left out.

8. Encourage your child to think well of himself. Evaluate what your child does well—maybe in-line skating, singing or dancing, working with animals, putting on skits—and encourage him in these efforts. Invite him to help other children in these activities.

9. Set an example by treating your child the way you want him to treat others.

Resolve

*I resolve to help my child stop her
mean teasing and bullying and interact
more positively with others.*

SMART TIP A child's bullying behavior can be frightening to a parent. Find a support group of other parents who have aggressive children and share your ideas and concerns.

section

③

ages 8–10

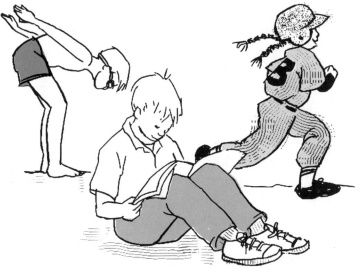

Example Behaviors

- Your fifth-grader watches TV or plays video games instead of doing his homework.

- Your child wants to watch TV instead of being with friends or doing other activities.

- Your ten-year-old views TV programs you disapprove of.

Thinking about It...

TV watching peaks during ages seven to eleven and then declines in early adolescence. During these earlier ages, children are still fairly home-based after school and on weekends. Many parents worry about the amount of TV their children view and about the increasing violence they see and hear. The debate rages on about whether watching violence on TV causes violent behavior. One thing is fairly clear: The more time a child watches TV in an unresponsive, passive way, the less time that child has for individual thinking and doing, using his or her imagination and creative abilities, and interacting with family members.

What to Say or Do

1. Give your child support for doing homework, projects, and activities other than viewing TV. For example, ask about your child's homework occasionally, encouraging her to explain the assignment or how it relates to what she's learning in class. Contribute comments, ideas, and household resources, when possible.

2. Use one of your child's TV interests to help her develop a new activity. For example, if she likes animal shows, she might enjoy putting together an animal scrapbook. If she prefers comedies or adventure shows, she might like to make up her own comedy or adventure and tell the family

about it. If she likes science shows, she might want to start a rock collection or do some simple experiments in the kitchen or her room.

3. Limit your own TV watching. Actively pursue your own interests at home other than watching TV.

4. Turn off the TV when no one is watching it. Don't let its noise compete for your family's attention during mealtimes and other family activities.

5. Set a specific limit for how much TV your child is allowed to view on schooldays and weekends.

6. Become aware of the programming options during the hours your child is at home. Determine which shows to encourage and which must be off-limits, and let your child know what these are.

7. Talk with your child, away from the TV, about the problem behavior. You might say, "I notice your TV watching is interfering with doing homework. You may decide when to watch TV—either after school or after dinner—but not both. If homework is not done, there will be no TV the next day. You decide."

8. Show an interest in the TV shows your child does watch and talk about them. Encourage your child to question what he sees and hears in the programming and the commercials. When children begin to have thoughtful responses to programs discussed in the home, they are more likely to be critical of media in general, including the shows you may disapprove of.

9. Encourage your child to invite a friend over for non-TV activities—decorating cupcakes or cookies, reading mysteries, riding bikes, or skateboarding. Some children enjoy starting a club with a few friends.

10. Try a ban on TV for the whole family for a stretch of seven days. Discuss your reactions with each other during and after the period. Encourage going to the library, playing outdoors, creating art, organizing a hobby, and so on.

Resolve

I resolve to help my child balance her day and ensure that her TV watching doesn't crowd out other activities.

SMART TIP   TV presents a complex variety of superb, so-so, and mediocre programming. Be on the lookout for potentially excellent specials and watch them as a family. When your child watches high-quality shows, he will become more able to recognize those that are substandard.

Example Behaviors

• Your son waits until the last minute to begin homework assignments.

• Your nine-year-old puts off doing her chores.

• Your child is always rushing to make it to the morning school bus.

Thinking about It...

Most children put off doing something until later on occasion. Frequent procrastination, however, can easily become a troublesome habit that is difficult to break. A variety of reasons lead children to procrastinate, including being easily distracted from the task at hand, being afraid of not doing well enough, and having a desire for more autonomy.

What to Say or Do

1. Talk with your child about his daily responsibilities that are getting pushed off until it's too late to get them done. Talk also about what he likes to do in his free time. Explain that paying attention to balancing "work" and "fun" activities is an easy way to help get everything done. Agree to work together to improve the balance of what gets done.

2. Some children appreciate having a routine so that they know exactly what is expected, in what order, and at what pace. Others want more flexibility and choices. If the more flexible schedule is chosen, be sure your child knows that when must-do activities such as homework or piano practice are put off on one day, any choice about what to do is eliminated the next day.

3. Help your child break longer projects into more workable pieces. Encourage progress on each small step and gradually show your child that she is actually accomplishing a great amount. This approach works well with long-term activities, such as a big school project or learning something new.

4. Limit reminders to your child to those things that need to be done fairly quickly, up to the next two hours, rather than also bringing up tasks that need to be done the next day and beyond. This approach will lessen your child's sense of having too much to do, make "I'll do it later" a less viable response, and help her focus on what needs to be accomplished now, in the moment.

5. Give reminders and offer encouragement and support to your child but do not actually do the task for him. You might say, for example, "This needs to be done now, Dan. Is there anything I can do to help you get it finished on time?"

6. Have your child organize her room and work space so it is easier for her to tackle tasks. Regularly help your child make sure that this space is well organized and conducive to getting things done.

7. Allow natural consequences for your child's procrastination. For example, your child's friends may not be able to come over if she doesn't give them enough notice. If homework is suffering because of procrastination, your child will get a lower grade. As needed, limit social and after-school activities so that the priorities are attended to first.

8. Show your child the positive consequences that result from completing tasks in a timely fashion. For example, point out how good it feels to have homework finished on time, and how much extra enjoyment a person feels during truly "free" time.

9. If getting ready for school on time in the mornings continues to be a problem, help your child organize details such as clothes, lunch, tickets, a note to his teacher, and so on the night before and be sure reasonable bedtimes are being met.

10. Establish the "now" habit. As a family, try to be on time and help each other be on time.

Resolve

I resolve to help my child get priority matters done on time, without procrastination.

SMART TIP

Create an orderly environment and a regular routine for your household. Such conditions are more likely to encourage your child's timeliness than when materials are scattered about or unavailable and the order of activities and schedules is frequently changing.

Example Behaviors

- Your child says he forgot to return his library books because his friend wanted him to play basketball.

- Your daughter insists she is late because of her sister's arguing.

- Your eight-year-old says, "I can't help it. It just happened."

Thinking about It...

One of the most common refrains parents hear when inquiring about a child's not taking care of a responsibility is "I forgot!" Learning to accept responsibility for one's behavior is a key aspect of becoming a mature and independent person. Many children, however, make excuses for their behavior, especially when they are trying to please and want to avoid criticism. As parents help children see that "I forgot" does not mean "and so I'm not responsible," they enable the children to acquire a sense of personal power and well-being.

What to Say or Do

1. Make sure your child knows that you love him even when he makes a mistake. Correct the behavior without criticizing or shaming your child.

2. Do not shift blame for your own mistakes to others. Be confident enough to say, "I didn't think this through very well, and I made the wrong choice." Let your children know mistakes happen to everyone. Then move on to talk about how to handle it. Help your child see that handling mistakes can be a learning opportunity.

3. Model the language of taking responsibility. Say, for example, "It's up to me to get this laundry done in time," or "I'm the one who will need to bring the keys."

4. Avoid becoming angry when your child makes a mistake. Anger will only reinforce your child's tendency to avoid taking responsibility because of fear of your disapproval.

5. When your child makes a mistake, calmly discuss the situation. What could he have done differently to have prevented the situation, if anything? What can he do now to make it better? What can be learned for the future? Use role play or play devil's advocate to help bring out new options and ideas.

6. When discussing your child's mistakes, be sure to talk about the consequences of various choices. You might say, "OK, good, we've thought of two other things you could have done in this situation. Now, for each of these, let's imagine how the consequences would have been different. What would probably happen next if you had chosen to do them instead of what you did?"

7. Listen to your child's explanation with an open mind when something goes wrong. Help your child be clear about the reasons for what happened. When all or part of the responsibility is hers, help her see that and freely admit it.

8. Help your child take personal responsibility by teaching him to make "I statements," such as, "I forgot to turn in my homework," or "I got angry and picked a fight on the playground." Then, encourage your child to make a commitment to improve his behavior.

9. Acknowledge your child for taking responsibility for her behavior. You might say, "I really appreciate it, Anna, when you are honest."

10. Let your child know that everyone makes mistakes and you don't expect perfection. The ability to see and admit a mistake is a great first step. The ability to correct and avoid repeating that mistake is yet another step. Be sure to encourage self-awareness and self-forgiveness in your child through the whole process.

Resolve

I resolve to help my child take responsibility for her own behavior rather than making excuses for it.

SMART TIP   Be sure your child knows the difference between reasons and excuses. A reason is an explanation for how and why something occurs. An excuse is an attempt to refuse to take responsibility, usually by blaming others.

MISTREATS BROTHERS AND SISTERS

Example Behaviors

- Your fourth-grader teases or provokes her brothers or sisters.

- Your child takes away siblings' toys or refuses to share toys, games, or computer equipment with them.

- Your son hits, kicks, or pushes his siblings.

Thinking about It...

Kids who fight with or mistreat siblings may be acting out of frustration, jealousy, hyperactivity, or a need for more parental attention or supervision. In most cases, such fighting is the children's problem, and parents can expect them to work out a solution. If children are fighting excessively or if someone is in danger of being hurt, the parent will need to step in and try to find and remove the underlying cause or separate them until their behavior improves.

What to Say or Do

1. Avoid taking sides with one of two bickering siblings. It is usually difficult to know the context of what happened. A useful approach is to help the two work out their issues by teaching them to resolve conflicts on their own. If they have been fighting over a toy or game, for example, you might take it away and help them come up with a plan for how to share it.

2. Treat all family members respectfully, and stress and expect that your children do the same.

3. Give an older child some responsibility for teaching something to her sibling. Such an activity can cultivate the sense of self-worth that comes from being a caring family member.

4. Discuss any ways in which your child feels frustrated in dealing with his siblings. Talk about alternative ways to deal with frustration, such as using words to express feelings instead of resorting to teasing or even violence.

5. Make sure your child has a private space and her own belongings that are off-limits to siblings.

6. Arrange to have plenty of support and help so that each of your children can have some of your time and attention. Enlist relatives, friends, or neighbors once in a while to help you with various tasks. You and your child can then go get an ice cream, for example, play catch in the backyard, or just spend a few minutes together talking at bedtime.

7. Explain to your child how others feel when they are teased. If possible, remind your child of a time when he was teased by others to help him recognize how bad this feels.

8. If your child physically hurts his sibling, enforce immediate consequences. Separate the children until he can conduct himself appropriately. When he is calm, encourage him to apologize and come up with a way to help his sibling feel better.

9. Acknowledge your child for treating siblings respectfully. Say, for example, "You're being very patient with your sister right now," or "I really like it, Megan, when you share with your brother."

10. For older children, encourage communication and problem-solving. Suggest they first have a cooling-off period. Then let them each state what they think happened. Have them tell each other how the situation makes them feel. Help them understand it's not possible to have what they want all the time. Have them suggest solutions. This process will take practice and patience. Continue to encourage them to work it out and avoid stepping in yourself.

Resolve

I resolve to help my children treat each other with respect and learn to resolve their conflicts through communication and problem-solving.

SMART TIP

Kids who mistreat siblings may feel competitive or be in need of special attention or new activities. Encourage your child's involvement with peers by having her friends over or making arrangements for outings with them. Participation in competitive sports can help your child release energy, blow off steam, and build confidence in her physical abilities—all while interacting with peers instead of siblings.

DOESN'T COMPLETE HOMEWORK SATISFACTORILY

Example Behaviors

- Your child has to be pushed or reminded to finish homework on time.

- Your daughter rushes through homework assignments, doing sloppy, careless work.

- Your ten-year-old begins but doesn't finish special projects for school.

Thinking about It...

Some kids resist doing homework, and they do so for a host of reasons: It's boring, it's too hard, it's not important, it's just worksheets, the assignment is too long, and so on. Schoolwork, of course, is the child's responsibility. The parent's role is to be supportive.

What to Say or Do

1. Encourage learning in general. Ask a lot of questions—about the weather, the seasons, how things work, plants and animals, people, TV shows, games, toys, sports, history, space, cooking, construction, creating things, and so on—and encourage your child to do the same. Brainstorm answers, ask friends and experts, consult books, look things up on the Internet. Enjoy the process of learning with your child.

2. Help your child be mentally alert. Give your child nutritious food, encourage daily exercise, and be sure she is getting enough sleep.

3. Tap into your child's natural curiosity. When your child shows interest in something, help him explore it himself, without giving him all the information you know about it all at once. Instead, be available, give a few facts if asked,

encourage his opinions, nudge his investigation here and there, and allow him to feel the excitement and satisfaction of acquiring knowledge.

4. Help your child establish a routine for homework. Have a specific place to do the homework, with good lighting and a comfortable chair. Give her a choice of when to do the homework—say, either before or after dinner. For example, your child might decide to start her homework around 4:30 P.M. (after an after-school snack and an hour of downtime, resting, or watching TV) and to finish around dinnertime at 6:00 P.M.

5. Talk to your child if he is having trouble with homework to find out what he thinks the problems are. Is he having trouble understanding the materials or ideas in class? Is he feeling insecure in some area? Take extra time to help your child make a plan to work on the problems.

6. If remembering assignments is a problem, help your child set up a system for tracking them. She might want to write down each assignment in a small daily planner and check off each one as it is completed. Or, if her school has such a system, she might take advantage of calling in to a voice message center that lists all current assignments for each grade.

7. Acknowledge your child and let him know you see his efforts when he does his schoolwork. You might say, "I have a lot of confidence in your ability, Leon. When you put your mind to it, you can really get this homework done on time—and correctly too!"

8. Become involved in several areas at your child's school to show her the value you place on education. Work occasionally on volunteer parent committees. Offer to help with field trips. Talk with your child's teachers about every six weeks to discuss her homework. Attend open houses, parent-teacher conferences, student performances, and so on.

9. To improve communication between your child and his teacher, you might see if your child and his teacher would be willing to trade journal entries, say once a week, on your child's homework. The child could make entries about his reactions to the assignment and doing it and the teacher could review the journal along with the assignments and then respond in the journal.

10. Help your child see the positive relationship between getting homework done and self-worth. You might say, "I can see by your smile that something is good here. I bet you know this B+ on your science test is a nice pay-off for all that hard work you did studying for it!"

Resolve

I resolve to support my child but not be responsible for her as she works on completing her homework assignments satisfactorily.

Resist the urge to jump in and *do* your child's homework—as, for example, when he is in a pinch with an impending deadline for a project. Show your support and encouragement in every way you can, but back off from any tendency to rescue. The more your child realizes you are letting him be responsible for his schoolwork, the more he will begin to handle that responsibility—or face the natural consequences at school.

Example Behaviors

- Your child responds rudely when you ask her to do something.

- Your son says you can't tell him what to do.

- Your ten-year-old endlessly argues or tries to negotiate when you state a rule or expectation.

Thinking about It...

Children test parental limits periodically—from infancy to adulthood—and children who are gaining more independence in their early elementary school years are no exception. Constant questioning of rules and limits can be wearing on parents. The challenge for parents of children who talk back at this age will be to keep an open, healthy climate in which discussion is acceptable but not if it turns disrespectful.

What to Say or Do

1. Acknowledge your child when she does not talk back to you. Say, "I appreciate it when you cooperate like this, Sofia," or "We can solve problems so much better when you speak respectfully."

2. Realize that some resistance and questioning is normal. As children gain independence and begin to think about fairness, their own viewpoints will surface and, inevitably, collide with some of yours.

3. Expect respect and give respect. Be polite to your child, spouse, and others. Kids usually speak to others the way others speak to them.

4. Consider letting some of your child's comments toward having the last word go unnoticed, as long as her tone of voice is respectful. Your child needs to learn to assert herself as she develops her opinions. As long as your child is not being rude, staunchly stated opinions can be taken in stride.

5. Halt the conversation any time your child is rude to you and do not tolerate obscene language or verbal abuse. End communication quickly by simply saying, "I won't listen to this language, Miguel. Let's cool off and get back together in five minutes." Or "When you change your tone, I'll be eager to hear what you have to say."

6. Model appropriate ways to question or disagree with rules to help your child learn alternatives to rude remarks. For example, use statements such as, "I have a different opinion," or "I'd like to say why I disagree with you."

7. If your child challenges your authority, calmly state your rule or expectation and, if needed, your reason. Avoid letting the interchange escalate into a shouting match or power struggle.

8. Even though your child may be rude to you, avoid shaming, criticizing, or using threats to stop or change the behavior. A more useful strategy is to be sure your child knows the difference between rude and respectful behavior. Then let him know that when he chooses to be rude, you will not respond, but when he is respectful, you will work with him to come to a solution.

Resolve

*I resolve to teach my child to respect
my decisions and to know how to
respond respectfully and appropriately.*

SMART TIP

If your child's rudeness is relatively new, consider whether she may be trying on the tone or attitude of her peers or someone on TV. Questions such as, "Hey now, where did you pick up this new attitude?" not only tell your child you notice but also remind her of the respect you are both more used to.

Example Behaviors

- Your daughter frequently complains that she is fat or ugly.
- Your nine-year-old is a perfectionist about his schoolwork.
- Your child thinks that she cannot do anything well enough.

Thinking about It...

Children who are critical of themselves are often struggling with self-esteem to some degree. Four commonly accepted components of self-esteem are personal significance (the child feels valued), competence (the child feels he can do some things well), power (the child has some influence over her own and others' lives), and purpose (the child has a sense of a future).

What to Say or Do

1. Tell your child how much you love and appreciate him every day. If children are to think well of themselves, they must feel valued, loved, and approved of by the people who matter to them.

2. Be honest with your child about the ways in which you are imperfect, so that she doesn't have an overly idealized image of you. You might say, "Sometimes, I give my opinion too quickly at work. I've been working on listening more closely before I speak."

3. Do not compare your child to his sibling or anyone else. Focus on the many ways in which he is unique and talented.

4. Be aware of your own expectations, especially those that may give your child the message that she isn't doing as well as she could be.

5. Help your child recognize and
   feel comfortable with his
   strengths. You might
   encourage your child
   to write down all of his
   finest qualities. Review
   and add to the list
   every month or so.

6. Help your child see that
   everyone makes mistakes sometimes.
   Help her move from unrealistic "I must be perfect" thinking to a more positive and productive understanding that
   includes, "I can learn from my mistakes" and "I'm getting
   better at [specific things]."

7. Let your child express his insecure feelings and acknowledge
   them. Just listen, without denying what he is saying. You
   might simply say, "It sounds as if you feel bad about yourself." After you are sure he knows you heard his feelings,
   you might say, "How can I help you see what a wonderful
   person you are?"

8. Help your child think about the power or advantage that
   can come by recognizing personal weaknesses. The power
   is in knowing who we are—our strengths and our weaknesses—realistically.

9. Acknowledge your child's efforts to accomplish things.
   You might say, "Hey, Maria, I see you've been keeping
   your room really neat!" or "I like the new hairstyles
   you've been trying out. Looks like you're having fun!"

10. Help your child plan ways to improve areas in which his confidence is low or his experience is limited. For example, he might decide to try building a simple model airplane to gain practice before tackling a more difficult model for his science project for school.

Resolve

I resolve to help my child see his unique gifts and support him in improving in areas in which he lacks confidence.

SMART TIP

Identify one area in which your child naturally excels and find ways for her to express this gift—for example, through art classes, volunteering, or participation in an extracurricular activity in which she can shine.

Example Behaviors

- Your child lies about completing homework or other tasks.

- Your third-grader lies about losing or damaging personal property.

- Your son exaggerates about his possessions to his friends.

Thinking about It...

Children in the elementary school years often exaggerate to bolster their own self-confidence. This embellishment of the truth is normal and usually fades as they begin to feel secure in the school setting. Some children lie to avoid disapproval or punishment. Children also lie to be accepted socially or to hurt someone else. Most children, by ages eight to ten, have a sense of morality. They feel wrong when they don't tell the truth and good when they do.

What to Say or Do

1. Do not punish so severely that your child fears telling the truth and risks lying.

2. Talk to your child as soon as possible if you think she has lied. Tell her in a direct, open manner that her story isn't believable and give her an opportunity to tell the truth. You might say, "I don't think you're telling the truth right now. Why don't you try it again?" or "Something doesn't ring quite true here, Ramon. Why don't you start over and tell me the whole story?"

3. If you suspect your child is lying, ask for a few details without accusing him. Too many questions, however, can put your child on the defensive and actually prompt him to lie to avoid a conflict. Instead of continued questioning,

state your thinking about a possible
deviation from the truth and encourage
him to be honest.

4. Do not lie to your kids or anyone else.
Even "little white lies" give kids the message
that lying is sometimes acceptable.

5. Periodically reassure your child that you
will love her regardless of her mistakes so
that she doesn't feel afraid to tell you the
truth. In most cases, kids begin to lie
because of fear.

6. If you find your child exaggerating
and suspect he is covering up feeling insecure,
let him know you know he is stretching the truth but avoid
making it an issue. Instead, work to help him build his self-
esteem and confidence. Spend some extra time with him
and acknowledge his talents and honest statements.

7. Be careful not to shame your child. If she has lied, simply
state the fact and the consequences. You might say, "I'm
disappointed in your choice, Michelle. I'm not disappointed
in you. I love you regardless of what you do."

8. Acknowledge your child when she tells the truth, especially
if doing so requires taking responsibility for behavior of
which she knows you disapprove. You might say, "You
can be proud of yourself for telling the truth about this,
Amanda," or "You took responsibility for yourself in a very
mature way."

9. If your child lies to other people (teachers, coaches, a neighbor, and so on), give him support and encouragement to clear up the situation with an immediate apology.

10. Explain to your child that a natural consequence of lying is that other people may not believe or trust a person after she has lied. You might want to read together the story "The Boy Who Cried Wolf," which illustrates this consequence well.

Resolve

I resolve to expect honesty from my child and to help her know that she can tell the truth and still be safe and loved.

SMART TIP

Foster open communication. Try to be as receptive and accepting as possible, so that your child will feel comfortable telling you the truth.

Example Behaviors

- Your daughter goes to her other parent when you say no.
- Your son tries to get what he wants by making comparisons, saying, for example, "But Mom lets me stay up late," or "Dad trusts me more than you do."
- Your child tells different versions of the truth to each divorced parent.

Thinking about It...

Kids who play one parent against another are looking for a weak link in the parents' relationship. Parenting, whether within single-parent, two-parent, extended, stepfamily, joint custody, or other family arrangements, needs clarity and consistency to be most effective. Communications naturally become more complex as more people and variations are added to the mix. The adults in the role of parent in one household need to speak as one voice to help keep the interactions as clear and simple as possible.

What to Say or Do

1. Determine mutually agreed upon rules and expectations with your spouse or partner. Expect to compromise to reach an agreement. If you are far apart in values, beliefs, or forms of discipline, seek professional help so that the two of you can be as consistent as possible in your parenting.

2. Be sure both parents are present when important issues are discussed with your child.

3. Don't put yourself in the position of explaining your spouse's or partner's feelings or position. Tell your child she needs to ask the other person directly.

4. Listen to your child's feelings, but don't acknowledge her criticisms of your spouse or partner. You might say, "I hear that you are angry at Dad, and I truly believe the two of you can work it out."

5. Be careful not to discuss your marital conflicts with your child. He should not be in the position of worrying about such issues or taking sides.

6. Have monthly meetings when every member of the family can air their feelings and concerns with everyone present. If this isn't workable, such as in a divorced situation with shared custody, try working with a professional counselor to improve communications.

7. If your child points out differences in parenting in a joint-custody situation, try to show cooperation and respect for the parenting in the other household, but stand firm in your own parenting. Children can usually adjust and learn to work with each parent's style.

8. Be prepared, if needed, to make adjustments in new step-parenting situations. Children who have difficulty accepting discipline from a stepparent may at first need to be disciplined only by the parent they are used to interacting with. Later, if the relationship grows and improves between the stepchild and stepparent, the discipline role can gradually shift to both parents.

9. If your child approaches you with a request for which you have no precedent, find out your spouse's or partner's position before giving your child an answer. If necessary, say, "Dad/Mom and I will need to discuss this together before I will be ready to respond." If possible, give your child a reasonable time frame so that she knows when to expect an answer.

10. Within the same household, support each other's authority. When one parent says, "No, you may not do that," it's essential for the other parent to stand by the decision. If you and your spouse or partner are in disagreement, work it out in private, not in front of your kids.

Resolve

I resolve to ensure that my child hears
a unified and fair parental voice.
To do this I will communicate well
with my spouse (or partner),
agreeing on our rules and expectations,
and support my spouse's authority.

SMART TIP

It's easy to feel flattered by kids seeing us as the nicer, better, or more sympathetic parent. Do your best to avoid creating alliances with your child by playing into favoritism.

Example Behaviors

• Your daughter demands clothes or a computer game that she desires.

• Your third-grader issues orders, such as, "Get me a sandwich."

• Your child frequently demands your immediate and undivided attention.

Thinking about It...

Self-centered, demanding behavior in children can develop when manners and respect are neglected, when parents are too responsive to or permissive with their children, or when appropriate roles and boundaries are not established for family members.

What to Say or Do

1. Avoid jumping into action every time your child wants or needs something. Teach your child that he can wait. Let him know that his new desires are not always the priority of the moment.

2. Encourage your child to be independent, whenever age-appropriate. When your child asks you to do something she could do for herself, suggest she do it. Offer help, as needed, the first few times. After she knows how to do something, make it clear it is now her responsibility.

3. Approach some contributions or activities in the family, such as folding and putting away one's own laundry, less as "chores" and more as practical, personal "responsibilities" to be done by each individual. Let your child experience the natural consequences that occur when he does not follow through with his part. His favorite shirt will remain in a wrinkled heap in the laundry basket, for example.

4. Do not be demanding toward your child. Ask your child to do things in a polite and considerate way. Use "please," "thank you," and "excuse me" when called for.

5. If your child demands certain products, acknowledge her desire and talk to her about how she might go about getting them. For example, if what she wants is appropriate, you might say, "Your birthday is coming up, Kristin. Let's put that video game on your wish list." Or "If you start saving your allowance this week, you'll be able to buy that new basketball in a month."

6. Make yourself available to your child so that he doesn't feel the need to demand your attention. Let him know when you will be able to listen and talk to him about what's on his mind.

7. Before going into amusement parks or museums and so on, remind your child of the consequences of being demanding. Let her know you will leave if necessary and follow through with this consequence.

8. Let your child know the budget for certain things. For example, in the area of clothes, you might say, "I've allotted $45 for blue jeans. If you want a more expensive pair, we'll need to come up with a way for you to earn the additional money."

9. Discuss what your child will be allowed to purchase before taking him shopping. Make it clear that there will be no further negotiation in public.

Resolve

I will help my child learn how to ask for what
he needs in a polite and respectful way.

SMART TIP

Don't give in to your child's demands out of feelings of guilt. It may be tempting to "make up" for other situations—for example, too much time spent away from kids—by indulging their demands, but doing so will only reinforce the demanding behavior.

Example Behaviors

• Your child complains or whines that she has nothing to do.

• Your son can't entertain himself without your participation.

• Your daughter can't stick to an activity without losing interest or becoming impatient.

Thinking about It...

Kids who are bored or discontent often need to find, build, and flex their own creative muscles. Some children take on a bored attitude from their friends because it seems like the "in" thing to do. Others are truly stumped for ideas and just need a few suggestions or someone to talk to for a few minutes. Unfortunately, overexposure to TV, movies, videos, arcade games, and the Internet can easily numb a child's ability to think, explore, investigate, and create on his or her own. When kids sit for hours in front of entertainment centers, they come to expect to be entertained or occupied by the next show, the next this, the next that.

What to Say or Do

1. Supply your child with a variety of art and craft supplies and various other materials with which she can do creative projects. If your child has a particular interest, say in bugs, help her be on the lookout for supplies and resources that relate to her interest.

2. Once your child is started on an activity, encourage him to finish it by himself. If his attention tends to flag, come by once or twice with questions and encouraging comments.

3. Encourage your child to start a collection, to research something in which she's interested, to repair something (or take it apart, figure out how it works, and put it back together), or to invent something.

4. Enlist your third-grader's help in figuring out fun and interesting things to do. When he is complaining there is nothing to do, for example, say, "Let's make a list of six fun and interesting things for you to do around the house and yard. Then you can pick one from the list to do for today."

5. Avoid "fixing" your child's boredom by immediately giving her something to do when she laments, "There's nothing to do around here!" Instead, ask, "What would you like to do?" If she insists on being bored, let her be "bored," but remind her she has the ability to create new activities, games, and so on whenever she wants to.

6. Be a good role model by filling your own life with varied activities, hobbies, friends, family, community activities, explorations, creations, and times of rest and relaxation.

7. Make sure your child gets plenty of physical exercise to use up energy in a healthy way.

8. Let your child know when you will be starting an activity of your own that will occupy your attention and suggest that he figure out what he'd like to do during that time.

9. Balance your child's free time with structured activities—such as nature walks or lessons in music, swimming, or judo—provided by her school or the community.

10. Encourage your child to read.

Resolve

I resolve to encourage my child to create her own activities and begin to develop her interests.

SMART TIP

Resist the temptation to resolve your child's complaints of boredom with the use of TV or videos. While putting your child in front of the TV or a video may provide a temporary solution, encouraging a passive activity will only teach your child to avoid being active and creative in finding constructive ways to entertain himself.

SECTION CONTENTS

BLAMES MISBEHAVIORS OR FAILURES ON OTHERS

Example Behaviors

- Your adolescent says, "Ming talked me into it," after he's been to an R-rated movie.

- Your daughter blames others for her poor performance at school, saying, for example, "My teacher didn't give the right instructions."

- Your sixth-grader blames his not coming home on time on you, saying, "You made me mad!"

Thinking about It...

Blaming others indicates an inability or unwillingness to assume responsibility for one's actions. Some of the reasons adolescents blame others include feeling insecure about their own abilities or decisions, being engaged in activities that aren't safe or that parents disapprove of for other reasons, and being intimidated by authority.

What to Say or Do

1. Do not expect more from your daughter than she can reasonably deliver. If your expectations are unjustifiably high, your child may feel she's in a no-win situation and blame others when she cannot do as well as you expect. On the other hand, give your daughter responsibilities that you know she can accomplish. Meeting responsibilities gives her a sense of self-worth and power that, in turn, makes it easier for her to admit mistakes.

2. When your son begins to blame someone else, refocus the conversation back to him by saying, "Let's talk about your part in this."

3. Take responsibility for your own mistakes. Let your adolescent witness how you shoulder blame and work through whatever steps must follow.

4. When your adolescent blames others, talk to her about how the mistake or problem could have been avoided. You might say, "You're blaming your teacher for giving you a poor grade, but I seem to remember that you only studied a half hour for that test. What might you have done differently, Kelly, to avoid that poor grade?"

5. Make sure your adolescent knows that while he may be disciplined for his misbehaviors, he is in no jeopardy of losing your love or approval by taking responsibility for such actions.

6. Explain to your daughter that mistakes give us the opportunity to learn and grow. When she makes a mistake, help her think through alternative choices and consequences. After the discussion, ask her what she has learned and what she feels. What will she do in the future if a similar situation occurs? Being armed with new and workable options usually helps a child feel empowered.

7. Be supportive as you help your son learn how to handle his mistakes or misbehaviors. You might say, "Well, the mistake is yours, Sergio, as you've just said. Let's talk about how you can solve it." By talking it through together, you are offering your presence and encouragement. This approach allows your son to feel your support and be more able to face what he needs to do.

8. Acknowledge your daughter when she takes responsibility for a misbehavior and does not try to blame someone else. Admitting blame for a mistake or misbehavior is hard. When your child does so, say, "It took courage for you to admit that, Dina," or "I see you are being strong and taking responsibility for what you did."

Resolve

I resolve to help my adolescent have the confidence and integrity to take responsibility for his misbehavior and mistakes.

SMART TIP   It can be difficult to be objective about our own kids. Avoid falling into the trap of allowing your adolescent to blame others because of your need to see her in a positive light. It's far more productive to hold your child accountable for her actions.

Example Behaviors

• Your son screams and yells at friends, siblings, and you when he's mad.

• Your adolescent uses loud name-calling or abusive language to express anger.

• Your daughter throws mini-tantrums when she doesn't get her way.

Thinking about It...

Adolescents have a powerful need to belong and fit in. As they navigate the sometimes choppy and unpredictable waves of getting along with friends, teachers, coaches, and others, their moods can soar happily one hour and take a nosedive the next. At the same time, their bodies and hormones are changing dramatically. Emotions can run high and are not always appropriately expressed. Even minor frustrations can precipitate intense reactions.

What to Say or Do

1. Let your adolescent know that it's perfectly OK to feel angry; it's just not OK to express the anger in a violent, raging manner.

2. Help your adolescent practice saying, "I'm angry right now because..." in a controlled, modulated voice. Getting used to naming the emotion and realizing that loud outbursts are not necessary or productive can be helpful.

3. Do not scream or yell at your adolescent or others. Children learn how to express anger primarily by how their parents communicate. Model healthy ways to handle your own daily stresses by, for example, getting enough

exercise and sleep, practicing relaxation techniques, not smoking, and not abusing medications or alcohol and other drugs.

4. Teach your daughter alternative ways of expressing anger. Talk about her feelings and concerns in a respectful way. She might try experimenting with writing down feelings in a journal or expressing them through an art form.

5. Help your adolescent recognize when he is angry by taking note of how his body feels. For instance, your son may be able to identify that his heart beats faster, his fists clench, or his jaw or stomach tightens up when he is angry. Being alert to these physical cues can help him realize what he is feeling in time to modify his reactions of yelling and screaming.

6. Acknowledge your daughter when she expresses anger appropriately. You might say, "Thanks for not blowing up by yelling and screaming. I can understand what you're angry about much more easily when you use this normal tone of voice."

7. Tell your adolescent you will not talk to her until her anger subsides and she settles down. You might simply say, "I cannot listen to you, Mary, until you're calm enough to talk more reasonably about this." Walk away or even leave the house, if necessary, to get this message across.

8. Be sure your adolescent restores anything he breaks or harms during a fit of anger.

Resolve

I resolve to teach my son how to express his frustrations and anger in a healthy and constructive way.

SMART TIP

Try to remain calm during your adolescent's outbursts. It's natural to react to screaming and yelling by screaming and yelling back. You may need to take some time in another room or leave the home to regain your composure before you can provide calm and confident support to your upset child.

Example Behaviors

- Your daughter keeps whining or pushing to get her own phone line.

- Your son repeatedly asks you "Why not?" when you've already said no and why.

- Your adolescent nags about almost everything—there's no peanut butter, her room is too dark, the headset is missing, and so on.

Thinking about It...

Children assert themselves in many ways against the pressures and confusion of adolescence. Facing new situations and expectations from teachers and friends takes its toll on them, and chronic nagging or whining in the safe haven of home can become a release valve. Other reasons for an adolescent's nagging or whining include frustration, unmet needs that he or she isn't able to express, simply being tired, and having unwittingly slipped into the behavior as a habit.

What to Say or Do

1. Tell your daughter that if she nags or whines, the consequence will be no attention or listening from you until she stops. Then do it. Wait her out by not responding. Be sure she sees the relationship between nagging and negative consequences. The more she nags, whines, or pushes, the less responsive you will be.

2. Be sure a *no* is necessary before giving one. Too many rules can beg resistance.

3. Stand firm on safety and other important issues, but consider being more flexible on less significant matters.

For example, you might always insist that your son wear a life jacket when waterskiing, but once in a while allow him to stay out an hour later than usual on a school night.

4. When your daughter begins nagging about one of your rules or decisions, have an open mind and consider whether her position is valid. Be willing to change your mind and, if you do, acknowledge that her point is a good one that you hadn't thought of earlier.

5. Listen to your son when he first makes a request and be sure he knows you have heard how he feels. You might say, "I hear that you're anxious about arriving at the pep rally on time. I have things to do, and I'll try to be ready to take you in about twenty minutes." Then try to follow through on your statement. If he begins nagging, say, "I won't be able to get ready, Tom, if you continue to nag me."

6. Be sure you explain your reasons well for the rules you have. Even though your daughter may not like a certain rule, she will be less likely to nag about changing it if she understands the reason for it.

7. Acknowledge your daughter when she does not nag. You might say, "Cally, I really appreciate it when you ask me quietly, clearly, and maturely."

8. Avoid letting your adolescent's nagging references to what another parent is allowing influence your decisions. Unless your child presents another parent's rationale for what he or she is allowing and that rationale makes sense to you and causes you to change your mind, your original decision is probably correct for your family. You might say,

"This is my decision for our family. Other families make their rules for their own families."

9. Talk about what to do as positive alternatives to nagging or whining. Ask your son to make requests reasonably by switching from a negative to positive tone and saying, for example, "Mom, the guys are all going to the mall tomorrow after school. May I go with them and get a ride home at 4:30?"

Resolve

I resolve to help my adolescent replace her nagging with requests and comments that are made more maturely.

SMART TIP Do not nag your adolescent. When your adolescent nags you, you can point out that you make a special attempt not to nag her about doing chores, homework, and so on, and you expect no nagging from her in return.

Example Behaviors

• Your adolescent questions almost every decision you make.

• Your seventh-grade son is belligerent toward teachers, coaches, or other authority figures.

• Your daughter accuses you of being outdated in your parenting.

Thinking about It...

Whether consciously or not, most adolescents have independence on their minds. They remember, and sometimes still yearn for and need, the easy protectiveness and dependence of their childhood. On the other hand, they now see glimpses of the more assertive, responsible, and independent aspects of their coming young adulthood. At various times, they feel excited and scared, hopeful and discouraged, challenged and thwarted. During this time of change, many adolescents struggle with how they relate to authority.

What to Say or Do

1. Be sure you and your spouse or partner agree on any rules you have. Support one another in enforcing consequences. If you are a single parent, get support from a friend for remaining consistent in your rules and consequences.

2. Let your adolescent know you are taking her thoughts and feelings into account before making a decision. You want your daughter to know that, although ultimately you have the final word, you are willing to listen to her.

3. Be clear and specific in explaining your decisions to your adolescent.

4. Stress the relationship between the rules you have and your adolescent's safety and well-being. Do not allow his anger or disagreement to sway you. You might say, "As your parent, José, it's my responsibility to make decisions that keep you safe, even when you aren't happy with them."

5. Avoid lengthy debates. Your adolescent will push you as far as you're willing to go. You might simply say, "I'm done discussing this now."

6. Give your adolescent gradually increasing involvement in decision making, according to his age and maturity. Help him think through the ramifications of his decisions, and be sure he is aware of the responsibilities that come with making a decision.

7. Help your daughter learn alternate ways to express her dissent. For example, suggest that she say, "I disagree with you," or "I really don't think the coach's decision is fair."

8. When you must hold to a decision in the face of your adolescent's anger, let him know when and under what circumstances, if any, your decision may change—for example, when he is a year older, or when he demonstrates responsibility in a related area.

Resolve

*I resolve to help my adolescent respect
and accept just authority.*

SMART TIP   Avoid defending yourself. Instead, remember that as the parent you have the right to exercise your authority.

Example Behaviors

- Your son's friends talk him into buying cigarettes for them, and your son is caught.

- Your daughter, who was supposed to be on a movie date, agrees to go out of town and ends up breaking curfew.

- Your son goes along with two friends who are slipping into a concert without buying tickets.

Thinking about It...

Peer influence is the social influence a peer group brings to bear on its individual members, as each member decides whether to conform to the expectations or whims of the group. Adolescents, who are often intent on belonging, can be extremely vulnerable to the influence of peers. Some adolescents cannot stand up to the taunting and teasing of peers; others succumb even without the jibes, as long as they can blend in with the crowd and not call attention to themselves. If not armed with strong refusal skills, adolescents can easily get caught up in going along with, giving in to, or being manipulated by others—even against their own better judgment.

What to Say or Do

1. Help your daughter say no by teaching her refusal skills. Encourage her to do the following:

   First, find out what you're getting into by asking questions.

   "Who's going to be there?"

   "What are we going to do?"

   "Are the parents going to be there?" (if going to someone's house)

Second, name the trouble to your friends.

"Well, you know that's shoplifting."

"Boy, if my mom catches me smoking, I'm grounded for the rest of my life."

"I might get an STD."

Third, suggest an alternative.

"I'm going to pick up a video. Would you like to come along?"

"Let's go play basketball."

Fourth, walk away. Leave the door open.

"Well, I'm taking off now. Come on over if you want to."

2. Do not act or speak against your own beliefs to please your peers. Assert yourself respectfully, as needed, in the workplace and in private and public social situations. Talk about some of these situations with your adolescent, when you think it might be useful.

3. Teach your son to be an independent thinker by encouraging him to form and express his own ideas. Foster dialogue and debate in your home to help your child learn how to assert himself and stand up for his viewpoint. Respect each other's ideas and opinions.

4. Discuss with your adolescent the potential dangers involved in not standing up to negative peer influence. Use real life examples to point out situations in which other kids have been hurt or even killed by doing what their friends wanted them to do.

5. If your adolescent uses the "But the whole gang did it, too" line of argument to persuade you to overlook misbehavior, say, "I'm concerned with you, not the whole gang," and "You're responsible for your own actions, no matter who else did it too."

Let your child know that there are no excuses for getting into trouble and consequences will follow.

6. Acknowledge your son each time he refuses to be affected by negative peer influence. Say, for example, "I noticed you weren't smoking after the movie, Al, even though two of your friends were."

Resolve

I resolve to help my adolescent withstand negative peer influence by encouraging her to build her own set of convictions and stand by them.

SMART TIP

Avoid overreacting when your adolescent talks about immature or dangerous behaviors of others. Being vulnerable to negative peer influence doesn't mean your young teen will act on it. Maintain a trusting, supportive attitude and encourage him to think about the consequences of that type of behavior. The possibility of real consequences is a powerful deterrent.

Example Behaviors

- Your son wears oversized, torn, or dirty clothing to school every day.

- Your adolescent doesn't bathe, shower, or brush her hair or teeth regularly.

- Your eighth-grader has her hair cut in an extreme style just before graduation.

Thinking about It...

Century after century, teens manage to carve out a new look for themselves. Distinct apparel (and sometimes attitude!) is usually part of adolescent culture. For some adolescents, "finding themselves" includes making new fashion statements. For many, expressing individuality in clothing, hairstyle, and grooming is a creative and fun pastime.

What to Say or Do

1. The older your adolescent is, the more say she should have in choosing clothing, accessories, and hairstyle. Don't become embattled unnecessarily.

2. Insist on good hygiene, regardless of your adolescent's style of dress, which may include some decidedly unconventional garb. Having a clean body, hair, and teeth are health issues, which you can expect your teen to respect.

3. Set standards for appropriate dress at different occasions and express your own individuality in dress, hairstyle, and accessories within those standards.

4. Tell your child you will not allow T-shirts or other clothing that advertises alcohol, tobacco, or other drugs or that contain racial, sexual, or religious slurs.

5. For certain significant occasions, such as a funeral, set guidelines for dress in advance. You might say, "For this occasion, your hair and clothing might seem disturbing or disrespectful to some. You'll need to modify them, but you can return to your personal look when it's over."

6. Do not allow clothing that projects a potentially dangerous signal, such as clothing that is sexually provocative or that reflects cult or gang attire. You might say, "This just won't do, Lynn, because this kind of dressing could endanger your safety."

Resolve

I resolve to allow my adolescent to express her personal style as long as she is relatively neat and clean and is not sending a disturbing or dangerous message.

SMART TIP

Avoid criticizing your adolescent's taste in clothing, accessories, or hairstyle as much as possible. Even if you find her style ugly, strange, or unflattering, criticism will merely increase distance between you. Keep your sense of humor. Remember, hair grows out.

Example Behaviors

• Your adolescent gives you one-word answers to questions.

• Your son tunes you out when you try to talk to him about what's going on at school, in sports or other activities, or with friends.

• Your thirteen-year-old daughter is sullen and unapproachable.

Thinking about It...

As adolescents continue to sort out their own identity and independence, many go through a stage during which they are uncommunicative, especially at home. Being physically and emotionally distant from other family members is common, and they may even become hypersensitive to simple everyday exchanges, such as, "Hi, how are you?" Knowing this stage is natural and typical can help parents weather the frustrating and sometimes distressing silences they may encounter with their son or daughter. Unless parents think a child's withdrawal indicates a larger problem—such as anger, depression, alcohol or drugs, or being afraid to tell them about something—they are often wise to simply allow the silence and not make it an issue.

What to Say or Do

1. Talk to your adolescent without expecting her to respond. For example, share something interesting about your day or comment on what's going on in the news. That way, she can just listen without having to interact and at least some communication has occurred.

2. Do not inundate your adolescent with questions. Kids sometimes stop talking because they're afraid that they don't have the right answer, and too many questions just further their withdrawal.

3. Keep reminders and instructions brief to avoid nagging. Sometimes just giving a cue will work well to remind an adolescent of a neglected chore or task. For example, instead of saying an entire sentence about remembering to feed the dog, just say, "The dog."

4. Let your son know that if something is bothering him you are ready to listen whenever he is ready to talk. You could say, "If you think it might help to talk, Ed, know that I'm here for you." If he wants to tell you something but doesn't want to talk about it, suggest he write you a note or letter instead of talking to you.

5. If her friends are reasonably mature, encourage your adolescent to talk to her close friends about something that might be bothering her. Kids appreciate it when parents understand the importance of peer support.

6. If you think your daughter might be hiding something or struggling to resolve something, suggest that she might find it helpful to talk with another adult—a teacher, school counselor, coach, relative, or friend. You might say, "Would it help if you talked to...?"

7. If your adolescent has been silent at home and doesn't go out much or talk on the phone, suggest that he write out or make a list of his thoughts, questions, or feelings to help sort things out. This approach can be particularly helpful for adolescents who don't have close friends or, for whatever reason, don't want to talk to them.

8. Ask your son if he is angry about something you have done and offer to listen. Young teens may stop talking as a way to "get back" at parents.

9. Write your adolescent a note or send a relevant greeting card with a short message if you're having trouble talking about something. Young people appreciate such gestures, as well as the effort and thought that goes into them.

Resolve

I resolve to take my cues from my adolescent about whether she wants to talk, unless I feel that her silence reflects problems that need professional intervention.

SMART TIP

Adolescents are sensitive to feeling intruded upon by parents. Be aware of how you phrase questions, taking care not to push your child to divulge more than he is comfortable sharing.

Example Behaviors

• Your adolescent condescendingly tells you to shut up.

• Your daughter uses profanity or obscene gestures.

• Your fourteen-year-old son barks, "Gimme that... " instead of saying please and thank you.

Thinking about It...

If you are a parent who is aggravated by an adolescent who is rude (aloof, condescending, abrupt, cynical, hypercritical, impolite, preoccupied, disrespectful, and so on), know that you are far from alone. Young teens can be masters at dishing out rude remarks and behaving discourteously. Underlying causes include minor stresses like a test at school, feelings of anger and frustration, and a need for attention.

What to Say or Do

1. Be sure your adolescent knows how you define rudeness. Be direct and be specific.

2. Let your child know how you feel when she is rude to you. You might say, "What you just said hurts," or "It makes me angry, Darletta, to be treated this way. We don't behave like this in our home. You'll have to do better than this."

3. Find out if your adolescent is angry or frustrated. Give him some slack if you know he is upset and dealing with some difficult feelings. Encourage your child to express his anger or frustration in a more constructive way, such as talking about it, or asking for help. Let him know you are available if he needs you.

4. Acknowledge your adolescent when he interacts with you or others respectfully. You might say, "I appreciate the gentle way you told your sister you couldn't help her."

5. If your adolescent acts outrageously rude in public, remove her immediately when possible and enforce consequences—even if doing so means going home in the middle of an event.

6. Keep your own behavior polite and respectful. When parents act rudely, kids get the message that they can act rudely too.

7. Help your son see that his rude behavior is his problem. When he shows disrespect to others, they know it, and he will need to take responsibility for that. Encourage him to think about what he has done and to apologize for it.

8. Let your adolescent know what you think of her friends' behavior when they are rude or use obscene language or gestures. If one of your daughter's friends barges into your house without knocking, teach that friend some house rules. You might simply say, "I want you to knock and wait for one of us before you come into our home."

Resolve

I resolve to help my adolescent be courteous and respectful to others.

SMART TIP

Leave the room if your adolescent is being rude and will not let up. You don't have to stick around if your child is being rude to you.

Example Behaviors

- Your son doesn't follow rules in public places. For example, he takes food into food-restricted areas, he ignores the lifeguard at the swimming pool, and so on.

- Your adolescent skips classes at school.

- Your daughter violates curfew and abuses telephone privileges.

Thinking about It...

Adolescents will break rules, and when they do, parents can respond with two simple reactions: Avoid becoming the nagging, critical, corrective parent, and hold your kid accountable.

What to Say or Do

1. Allow your adolescent to experience natural consequences when she breaks rules outside the home. Do not rescue her or intervene to lessen the consequences. For example, if your daughter is chastised by your neighbor for picking his flowers, you might discuss it with her but be sure she's the one who figures out how to make up for the wrong and does so.

2. Set an example by following rules yourself, including rules at home, at work, in sports and other activities, and in public places.

3. Make sure your adolescent understands the rules that apply to him and the reasons for them. Avoid nagging constantly. Instead, use the family meeting to discuss concerns about broken rules and to negotiate.

4. Stress that your knowing your adolescent's whereabouts is for your benefit. You might say, for example, "Calling home when you go somewhere assures me that you are safe. Otherwise, I get worried." This teaches adolescents to be aware of other people's feelings.

5. Clearly define the direct relationship between breaking rules and logical consequences. For example, "If you leave your bike out and I have to put it away, you will not be allowed to ride it tomorrow." Or "If you skip classes and fail science, you'll be required to go to summer school instead of going to camp."

6. Acknowledge your adolescent for following the rules. Say, for example, "I really appreciate that you called, Rosa, and let me know where you are."

7. Create a written contract with your adolescent in which she agrees to follow certain rules. For example, "I, Julie, agree to be home by 10:30 P.M. on weekends." Written contracts help some youngsters assume more responsibility for their actions. The contracts help parents point out infractions, for example, "Tim, you signed the contract, indicating you agreed to be home by 10:30 P.M. Since you were fifteen minutes late tonight, you'll have to come in thirty minutes earlier tomorrow."

8. If your son breaks rules at school, meet with his teachers, school counselor, and principal, if appropriate. Support the school in carrying out its consequences. Work with your son to see that he doesn't repeat these actions.

Resolve

I resolve to see that my adolescent follows the rules necessary for her safety and well-being.

SMART TIP Avoid jumping to conclusions. Let your adolescent explain what happened. Be sympathetic while holding him accountable for his actions.

Example Behaviors

- Your adolescent frequently skips English class, saying it's boring and irrelevant.
- Your son doesn't study and is performing below his academic ability.
- Your daughter and her peers think "school's not cool."

Thinking about It...

Some children begin to have difficulties academically when they move from elementary school to middle or junior high school. Naturally, these difficulties worry parents, who know that high school and careers loom just around the corner. Struggles over homework usually peak during this period. The young teen, faced with more teachers and classes and longer assignments, can be overwhelmed with the expanded academic, social, and emotional demands of this time. A practical and healthy approach for all concerned is to keep the focus on developing a strong, positive attitude toward learning—in all its forms—rather than getting too hung up on specific grades and immediate results.

What to Say or Do

1. Occasionally ask about your adolescent's understanding of the main ideas in her assignments. Be available to stimulate interest and clarify any confusion. Help your child see that her comprehension of concepts and operations is often far more important than memorizing, and be sure she seeks help from her teachers as needed.

2. Read and learn yourself as much as possible—for information and for enjoyment. Comment on what you are learning.

3. Help your adolescent create an area for doing his homework and personal projects. You might say, "Tory, now that you're in junior high, you need a regular place for doing your homework and other projects. Let's fix up a space for you." Be sure he has a desk or table, a comfortable chair, a lamp, and any needed notebooks, reference books, art supplies, and so on.

4. Set clear rules about homework with your adolescent, with the understanding they will be reviewed and possibly modified after each grading period. The rules should outline regular study times and set limits on after-school activities such as watching TV, telephoning, going places, and having friends over.

5. If your adolescent's grades are slipping in one or more subjects, approach the topic with care. Too much pressure and nagging can worsen the situation. Mention your concern, and give your daughter some time to improve on her own. Acknowledge signs of effort and improvement. If underachieving continues, make an appointment to meet with your child and her teachers to clarify expectations and get some additional guidance about what to do. The sooner you seek help the easier it will be for your daughter to get back on track.

6. Encourage studying with one or two friends for major tests. Small group studying can work well at this age and can alleviate some of the related anxiety, dread, and even procrastination.

7. Encourage critical thinking about the material your adolescent is studying by encouraging him to question it. Are the sources reliable? What other viewpoints exist? Can he think of some ways to test the validity of what he's learning? Urge him to ask his teachers and others about any questions he has.

8. If your adolescent's attitude is negative about schoolwork or school in general, encourage her to think about what the problem is. You might say, "I don't understand this new attitude, Vanessa. What would it take to be a little more positive toward school? Can you find any connections between what's important to you and what you can get from school?" She may not have the answer immediately, but with some space to think about it she may figure it out. Usually kids who think that school's "not cool" come to realize that doing well in school actually helps them meet their most personal goals—knowing more, getting a better job, getting into college, and so on.

Resolve

I resolve to help my adolescent value learning and be self-motivated to meet life's challenges.

SMART TIP

Do not rescue your child by doing her homework, but at times participate in a project or assignment to a certain extent. For example, if your child is to write a report on a book, you would not write the report. You might, however, read the book after your child has done so and talk over funny, odd, or interesting parts.

Example Behaviors

• Your son smokes cigarettes or chews tobacco.

• Your daughter's eyes are red, and she is more talkative and excitable on occasion when she comes in at night.

• Your twelve-year-old is caught with marijuana in his school locker.

Thinking about It...

Tobacco, alcohol, and many other drugs are inexpensive, easily available to young people, and highly destructive to an adolescent's developing body. And they're everywhere—at parties, on the street, in the parking lot, at the mall, at school. Any use by kids is high risk, and parents need to be deeply concerned and take clear, firm action to address it.

What to Say or Do

1. Clearly and often tell your adolescent your expectations that she not use tobacco, alcohol, or other drugs. State these every time she goes out. With her, decide what the consequences will be should you have any evidence or suspicion of alcohol or other drug use.

2. Learn about tobacco, alcohol, and other drugs. Even if your adolescent appears in no danger of using chemicals, a shift in emotions, peer influence, sudden availability, and countless other situations can change that rapidly. Be prepared with knowledge.

3. Set a good example about health and safety by not abusing tobacco, alcohol, or other drugs. Talk to your adolescent about why you make the decisions you do about tobacco, alcohol, or other drugs.

4. Set a reasonable time for your son to be home. Be awake and interact with him when he comes home.

5. Talk with your adolescent in advance about situations that may lead into use of tobacco, alcohol, and other drugs. Together, discuss ways to avoid such situations. For example, if older kids bring alcohol in cars to have outside during after-game dances, help your young teen make a plan to stay inside or near the building and not go into the parking lot.

6. Help your adolescent learn to resist any drug use by teaching her refusal skills (see pages 93–94 of this book).

7. Give your adolescent accurate information about alcohol, tobacco, and other drugs. Simple, clear pamphlets and bulletins can be acquired from hospitals, treatment centers, and school counseling offices. Materials are available on the Internet.

8. If your young teen is using tobacco, do not allow it in your home or vehicles or in your presence.

9. Know where your adolescent is going. Kids will often ask to spend the night at a friend's house when they plan to use. Tell your son in advance that you'll be checking up. Then do it. Talk to the hosts of an event or party and ask if alcohol or tobacco is allowed and to what degree the hosts plan to be involved. Ask the same questions of the parents of any friend with whom your son wants to spend the night. Make sure he's where he says he will be.

10. If your son develops a problem with tobacco, alcohol, or other drugs, do not hesitate to take him to a professional in alcohol and other drug issues for an assessment to find out the extent of the problem and how to remedy it.

11. Your kids have a hot line of communication. Develop one among parents too.

Resolve

I resolve to help my child be prepared to make healthy decisions around situations that might involve using tobacco, alcohol, or other drugs.

SMART TIP

If your intuition tells you something is wrong, it probably is. Trust your perceptions.

section ⑤ ages 15–18

WON'T PARTICIPATE IN FAMILY ACTIVITIES

Example Behaviors

- Your son wants to eat in front of the TV or in his bedroom instead of with the family.

- Your teenager refuses to attend family gatherings.

Thinking about It...

Most teenagers go through a stage during which they would prefer not to spend time in family activities. Don't panic if your child argues against going to some dinners or social gatherings of the extended family. Such behavior is typical and does not necessarily signal other problems.

What to Say or Do

1. Make family events as enjoyable as possible by keeping conflict to a minimum.

2. Specify what is and isn't mandatory for your teen to participate in. For example, you might agree that your son must eat Sunday night dinner with the family but doesn't have to come to the quarterly neighborhood block parties. Or you might insist on participation on important holidays such as Christmas or Hanukkah and at certain weddings, funerals, and other significant life-cycle events, but let the more routine affairs be optional.

3. Allow your teen to invite a friend to family activities. Many teenagers are more willing to participate when a peer is included.

4. Invite your teen to suggest family activities he would enjoy and follow through on some of his suggestions.

5. If a family event is mandatory, let your teenager know how long she will be expected to participate. Don't say, "We'll be at Grandma's for about an hour," and then stay three hours.

6. Encourage your teenager to bring along something—homework, a book or a video game, cards—when you attend family gatherings that are likely to last several hours.

7. Try to host some gatherings of your extended family at your home so that your teen can participate for a while and then spend some time doing other things in her own room.

8. Stress a respect for the elderly. Make sure that your teen understands the importance of spending time with grandparents.

9. Don't insist that your teen sit with you at church or other family events. Allow her to sit with friends or relatives her own age.

Resolve

*I resolve to let go of expecting my teenager
to participate in every family activity,
but I will firmly expect her attendance
at specified significant events.*

SMART TIP This type of behavior has nothing to do with you. It's the rare teenager who chooses family time over time with friends.

Example Behaviors

- Your teenage son lies about where he is, has been, or is going.

- Your daughter lies to cover up her driving with no license.

- Your fifteen-year-old son cheats on tests at school and when playing games with friends.

Thinking about It...

Teenagers will lie about their misbehaviors. Usually they do so to protect themselves from disapproval, embarrassment, or the anticipated consequences. Kids lie and cheat when they don't believe their best is good enough and they feel pressure to perform at a higher level. Sometimes teens are trying to cut corners and get by without putting in the required effort. Sometimes they lie to avoid hurting a friend's or a parent's feelings; they don't want their misbehaviors to let the person down. Fierce competitiveness can lead teens into lying and cheating.

What to Say or Do

1. Be informed. Be aware of your teenager's whereabouts by making sure that he checks in by phone regularly. Talk to your son's teachers and coaches, usually once per grading period, to have a general awareness of his performance and attitude at school. Interact with his friends and their parents. Merely being "in the loop" in this way lessens your teen's ability to con you.

2. Be honest. Do not cheat or lie yourself.

3. Be sure your teenager knows that nothing she does, even if it brings on negative consequences, will diminish your love.

4. Check out the facts. Don't confront your teenager with a lie or cheating without proof. On the other hand, if you know your child is lying or cheating, say so matter-of-factly.

5. When your teenager lies about something and gets caught, let's say driving without a license, let her know that lying has compounded the problem and increased the consequences. You might say, "Your ticket's the natural legal consequence for driving with no license, and you'll have to pay it. In the meantime, I want you to stay home next weekend because you decided to lie to cover it up. The week after that you'll have a chance to tell the truth about whatever you choose to do."

6. Look for ways to open the lines of communication with your teenager. If your teen is lying, perhaps he doesn't feel safe telling the truth. Ask him whether he feels a threat from you or anyone, which makes telling the truth difficult.

7. Instead of dwelling on your teenager's lying or trying to hide a situation, emphasize finding a solution. Once your initial anger or exasperation is under control, you might say, "Carrie, your nail polish remover has taken the finish off the table. I'm quite upset, but I'll get over it. The important questions for you now are how are you going to repair the table and how can you prevent this from happening again?"

8. Be sure your teenager is aware of the natural consequences of cheating, such as getting a failing grade, not understanding important information, losing friends, being fired at work, and so on. If she cheats anyway, allow her to experience those natural consequences. Talk to her about whether whatever was gained by cheating was worth the consequences.

9. Work on building your teen's self-esteem. It's fine to acknowledge his natural talents and the new skills he is learning. Focus primarily, however, on helping your son know that he's OK as he is—without doing anything special—with his weaknesses as well as his strengths. Teens usually don't want to lie, and when self-esteem is strong, it is easier to admit a mistake.

10. Let your teenager know that you want to be informed if bad news is coming. You might say, "Things will go much better for you, Eric, if you tell me about something before I hear it from the police, school, or neighbors. I don't like surprises."

Resolve

*I resolve to help my teenager see that
honesty is the best policy.*

SMART TIP Encourage family discussions of the double standards in our society and ethics in general. Teens are keenly aware of manipulation, injustice, and hypocrisy. Help your teen make telling the truth a strong value.

Example Behaviors

- Your teenage son is spending time with another teen who just dropped out of high school.

- Your daughter sometimes hangs out with kids who are using alcohol and other drugs.

- Your teen is involved with some kids who often get in trouble at home and at school.

Thinking about It...

A teenager's friends are usually a source of companionship, support, and fun. Unfortunately, friends can sometimes be negative influences. When a teen is drawn to others who are involved in unhealthy or destructive patterns, one or more of the following factors may be operating: having a perceived need to be tough or sexy, seeking danger or risk for its thrill, rebelliousness, or anger.

What to Say or Do

1. Encourage your teenager to invite her friends, including new ones, to your house. Let your daughter know that you like to meet them and observe their attitudes and behavior. If your teen refuses to have a specific new friend over, this can indicate that she knows you might object to this friend.

2. Be careful not to base any objections on the appearance of your teenager's new friends. It's hard to accurately judge a child by his appearance. Focus only on behavior or attitudes that are not safe or appropriate. For example, in stating your reasons for disapproving of a certain friend, you might say, "I don't like you hanging out with Ray because he's been found guilty in juvenile court at least

twice—once for drinking and once for trespassing." Stress your concern for your child's safety.

3. When your teenager seems to be shifting to new friends, encourage her to maintain or renew ties with at least one or two of her more long-standing friends. Keep up communications with the parents of those friends to discuss concerns, including any about new friends.

4. Tread lightly when asking questions about your teen's new friends. Teenagers can be particularly touchy about their friends, perhaps because of their close link with choices and independence. Similarly, belonging, hanging out, and being cool are intensely personal endeavors to teens, and they often resent a parent's questions about those with whom they are choosing to spend time.

5. If your teenager dismisses his former friends as boring, uptight, snobby, or whatever, take the opportunity to find out about how his interests and attitudes are changing. You might ask, "What do you like more about being with this new crowd than with your old friends?" Or "What intrigues you about these new friends? What new directions do you see for yourself in being with these new friends?"

6. Trying to pick your teenager's friends is futile. Consequences speak more loudly than a parent's caution. You can rely on this to turn a teen around. Be sure to continue to consistently enforce the household rules that protect your child's health and safety—for example, coming in at a reasonable hour and no use of alcohol or other drugs.

7. Calmly point out changes in your teen's attitude or behavior. Stick to the facts. Say, "I expect this behavior to change." Clearly state the consequences if it does not. If the behavior continues, put the consequences in effect.

Resolve

I resolve to encourage my teen to make friends with others who behave responsibly and safely and to avoid those who don't.

SMART TIP — Think twice about forbidding your teen-ager to associate with kids who have a bad track record. Such an approach can easily backfire. Kids often dig their heels in harder in the face of parental disapproval.

Example Behaviors

• Your sixteen-year-old daughter is hypervigilant about her physical appearance—her hair, skin, nails, makeup, clothes and accessories, weight, posture, gait, body language, and voice.

• Your teenage son spends almost all of his free time working out and spending money on fitness equipment, vitamins, and supplements.

• Your teen weighs and measures herself every day, tries one diet after another, and is depressed about her body.

Thinking about It...

It's natural for teenagers to be extremely focused on their appearance. Their bodies are still undergoing dramatic changes that began in puberty. They want to fit in and be accepted, and looking "good"—however that is defined for them—is a huge issue.

What to Say or Do

1. Talk with your teenager about body image and self-worth. Be sure that she knows that a positive body image comes from within, not from ratio of body fat to muscle, bone structure, or certain clothes or hairstyles.

2. Help your teenager focus on aspects of himself, such as talent, intelligence, or mastery of various skills, not related to his looks. You might remind him, "Your intelligence is awesome to me," or "When are you going to teach me how to pitch like that?"

3. Encourage your teenager to see that the "ideal" or "perfect" look perpetuated by fashion magazines, models on runways, music videos, billboards, and so on has its skewed and

extreme aspects. Discuss the ways overly thin or muscled bodies might be unhealthy.

4. Keep lots of nutritious, fresh foods on hand for the family's meals and snacks.

5. If your teenager has a continuing physical condition that affects appearance and might be embarrassing, such as crooked or missing teeth, severe acne, or eczema, try to provide medical treatment, if financially possible.

6. Make sure your teenager gets plenty of exercise. Working out or participating in athletic activities strengthens your teen's body, relieves stress, and improves self-esteem.

7. Help your teenager appreciate her own unique beauty. Point out particular physical qualities that enhance her appearance. You might say, "Juanita, you have a beautiful smile." Other qualities might be tone of voice, gracefulness, coordination, warmth, peacefulness, or sense of humor.

Resolve

I resolve to encourage my teenager to accept herself as she is and to know that she is loved no matter what her appearance may be.

SMART TIP

Don't let your own appearance become an issue in your life. If your appearance is your priority, your teen's preoccupation with hers will be almost ensured.

ACTS SELFISHLY AND WON'T HELP AROUND THE HOUSE

Example Behaviors

- Your sixteen-year-old complains and stalls when you ask her to help vacuum and dust.
- Your teen needs to be the center of attention and seems oblivious to other people's feelings.

Thinking about It...

Keeping a household clean and orderly is not a priority for most teenagers. Let your teen know that chores and other household maintenance are one of those can't-get-away-from-it realities of life. Acting selfishly sometimes means a teen is afraid that there is a scarcity of resources—time, money, or love. More often, it's thoughtlessness that can be remedied with broadened awareness.

What to Say or Do

1. Let your teen be aware of all the work, meetings, and other engagements you have throughout the week. Likewise, acknowledge all his activities, including school, studying, working, being with friends, sports, and just hanging out. Together, talk over the value of maintaining a clean and orderly household and note that you each depend on the other's contributions and cooperation. You might say, "We need each other around here. I expect each of us to do our fair share."

2. Demonstrate generosity—with smiles, hugs, time, small gifts, encouragement, attention, sympathy, and ideas. Give freely of yourself to your partner, your child, and those around you. Make charitable giving and volunteering a family tradition.

3. Expose your teen to the real world. Don't shelter him from poverty, hunger, or homelessness. Discuss the plight of those in need and share ideas of how to help.

4. Keep a list of all recurring household chores and ask your teenager to choose three or four that she will be responsible for. A change in selections can be made with each new season. Make less frequent chores, such as raking a large lawn or cleaning out the attic or garage, a special event by having the family do them together, perhaps followed by a video and pizza or dinner out at a restaurant. Your teen may want to invite a friend over for such a chore-and-treat day.

5. Do not allow your teenager to monopolize family conversations or activities. Help her to see that each member of the family has equal time.

6. When your teenager acts selfishly, find out if he's feeling bad about anything. People, including adults, are more prone to act selfishly when they are feeling scared or angry.

7. Take time as a family to give thanks for all you have. Talk with your teen about appreciation for necessities, comforts, and most of all, each other.

8. Expect a certain amount of self-centeredness in your teen. Teenagers are preoccupied with finding out who they are. Along these lines, allow your teen to have her own messy room if you can.

Resolve

I resolve to help my teenager do her fair share toward maintaining an orderly household and to be generous with her time and possessions.

SMART TIP

Don't nag your teen about household chores. If necessary, let his laundry pile up until the consequence of having no clean clothes for something important begins to bug even him. Natural consequences are often much more effective in changing a negligent pattern or attitude than a parent's nagging.

IS SEXUALLY ACTIVE

Example Behaviors

- Your seventeen-year-old daughter breaks curfew often to be out late with her boyfriend.

- You find birth control pills or condoms in your teen's room or bathroom.

Thinking about It...

Teenagers face enormously conflicting messages about sex, an emotionally charged topic that our culture glorifies. As teens form their sexual identities, they have many choices, including experimenting with sexual activity, withdrawing from it altogether, postponing it, and becoming sexually active. Confusion, doubt, excitement, pleasure, fear, and wonder are just a few of the emotions about sex they will probably experience during this time.

What to Say or Do

1. If you feel awkward talking to your teenager about sex, start out by saying just that. You'll probably get your teen's respectful attention by saying, "It's uncomfortable for me to talk about sex with you, but you're important to me. I love you, and I think we should talk about it once in a while. Are you OK with trying a few short talks?" If your teen agrees, have a topic ready, such as the pressures to be sexually active, and make one comment about it and ask one question. Keep it casual and short. Once the door is opened, you'll be surprised how much easier talking about the subject will become.

2. Encourage your teen to talk about sex whenever he has questions or concerns. Let him know you understand the pressure to be sexually active is great and you support

him in making informed decisions that make sense for his own well-being.

3. If your teenager has trouble talking to you about the physical, emotional, or other aspects of sex, encourage her to talk to someone else who is knowledgeable. Let her know you support her in every way, no matter what the trouble or concern is.

4. Help your teenager be informed about sex. Be sure he has access to accurate reading material. If you have not already done so when your child was in junior high, enroll in a sex education workshop for parents and teens. See that the sexual education covers the physical and emotional aspects and the responsibilities and consequences.

5. Discuss the huge consequences that can come with sex, including babies, sexually transmitted diseases, and the effect they may have on one's future job, further schooling, travel, and so on.

6. Caution your teen about the possibility of being rejected after having sex and the deep emotional hurt that follows.

7. Discuss the reality and alarming frequency of date rape with your teen. Remind her that alcohol is usually involved in these cases and talk about how to avoid such situations. Be sure to caution her about the potent tranquilizer Rohypnol, illegal in the United States but used in some date rapes. You might say, "Never take a beverage from someone you don't know, Shelly, and don't let it out of your sight."

8. Talk to your teenager about standing up for his values and respecting himself. (If needed, help him learn to resist pressure by teaching the refusal skills found on pages 93–94 of this book.)

9. Discuss with your teen types of intimacy, such as spirituality, sharing common goals, and enjoying doing things together. Assure her that working on building a mature, solid, and caring relationship with another person can bring a lifetime of fulfilling experiences.

10. Let your teen know that you prefer he is not sexually active until he is older or married, if that is your family standard. Explain that you want him, before he decides to have sex, to be in a committed relationship.

11. Provide the appropriate health care for your teen if he or she is sexually active.

Resolve

I resolve to help my teenager make an informed decision about when to become sexually active.

SMART TIP

Don't wait until you suspect sexual activity or have a crisis on your hands to talk to your teen about sex. Remember, the talks don't have to be serious, seminar-like marathons. Set a relaxed atmosphere where comments on developments in AIDS research or concerns about a friend who is pregnant can help broaden the context.

Example Behaviors

• Your teen breaks windows and sprays graffiti at the high school.

• Your teenager is part of a brawl at a party.

• Your teen and another are caught trespassing and egging a friend's house.

Thinking about It...

Teenage vandalism and violence are on the rise. Heart-breaking, murderous shootings of teens by teens are happening in North American junior high and high schools. TV and news magazines report story after story of violence by young people. Gang activity, formerly centered in inner cities, has spread to suburban and farm communities. Unfortunately, warning young people of the dangers all around them has become a part of responsible parenting.

What to Say or Do

1. First, sit down with your teenager and listen to his description of what happened.

2. Clarify the risks. Point out that vandalism and violence can lead to some serious consequences, including getting wounded or even killed, having a police record, getting sued, getting expelled from school, getting fired from a job, and not qualifying for college or jobs because of a record.

3. Concentrate on having your teenager make restitution. Be sure she thinks through and carries out a sensible way to make things right, which may include cleaning up the mess, making repairs, paying bills, and apologizing.

4. Check if your teenager is getting into trouble elsewhere—at school, on the job, in athletics. Follow up, as necessary, if a larger picture opens up.

5. If you suspect your teenager may be in a gang, get help immediately. Locate gang intervention specialists and begin family counseling. Do not try to deal with this without support.

6. Teach your teenager how to handle violence without being violent. Help your teen learn how to remove herself immediately from situations that may turn or have turned violent. Be available to pick up your child should he need to leave a situation.

7. Fighting and vandalism are often linked with alcohol and drug abuse. If you suspect there's a connection, do not hesitate to have a professional evaluate the extent of the problem and recommend steps to take.

Resolve

I resolve to help my teen steer clear of violence and destruction—to others and to property.

SMART TIP

Work with other parents to urge school and community officials to establish more teen centers with programming and activities related to teen interests and issues. Volunteer to help out on planning committees at teen centers and encourage improvements that give teens healthy choices.

Hazelden Information and Educational Services is a division of the Hazelden Foundation, a not-for-profit organization. Since 1949, Hazelden has been a leader in promoting the dignity and treatment of people afflicted with the disease of chemical dependency.

The mission of the foundation is to improve the quality of life for individuals, families, and communities by providing a national continuum of information, education, and recovery services that are widely accessible; to advance the field through research and training; and to improve our quality and effectiveness through continuous improvement and innovation.

Stemming from that, the mission of this division is to provide quality information and support to people wherever they may be in their personal journey—from education and early intervention, through treatment and recovery, to personal and spiritual growth.

Although our treatment programs do not necessarily use everything Hazelden publishes, our bibliotherapeutic materials support our mission and the Twelve Step philosophy upon which it is based. We encourage your comments and feedback.

The headquarters of the Hazelden Foundation are in Center City, Minnesota. Additional treatment facilities are located in Chicago, Illinois; New York, New York; Plymouth, Minnesota; St. Paul, Minnesota; and West Palm Beach, Florida. At these sites, we provide a continuum of care for men and women of all ages. Our Plymouth facility is designed specifically for youth and families.

For more information on Hazelden, please call **1-800-257-7800**. Or you may access our World Wide Web site on the Internet at **http://www.hazelden.org**.